VILLAGE SCHOOL DOWNTOWN

By the author of VOICES IN THE CLASSROOM

VILLAGE SCHOOL
DOWNTOWN

POLITICS AND EDUCATION–
A BOSTON REPORT

BY PETER SCHRAG

Beacon Press · Boston

The author wishes to thank the following for permission to reprint copyrighted material: The author and The Atlantic Monthly Company for excerpts from "The White Northener: Pride and Prejudice," copyright © 1966 by The Atlantic Monthly Company, Boston, Mass. 02116; reprinted by permission. Excerpts from *A Teacher Speaks* by Philip Marson, copyright © 1960 by Philip Marson and used by permission of David McKay Company, Inc. Excerpts from *The American Irish* by William Shannon, reprinted with permission of The Macmillan Company © 1963 by William V. Shannon. "I Have A Rendezvous With Death" is reprinted with the permission of Charles Scribner's Sons from *Poems* by Alan Seeger; copyright 1916 by Charles Scribner's Sons, renewal copyright 1944 by Elsie Adams Seeger.

A brief portion of *Village School Downtown* was first published in *Saturday Review*.

FOR JANE

ACKNOWLEDGMENTS

THIS BOOK could not have been written without the cooperation and support of many individuals inside and outside the Boston School Department, and without the tolerance and encouragement of my colleagues at Amherst College. Superintendent William H. Ohrenberger graciously granted me permission to visit the schools, and many members of his staff were helpful in providing information. I am also indebted to Dr. Robert Coles, research psychiatrist at Harvard University, Diane Divoky of the *Boston Herald*, Bertram Waters and Ian Forman of the *Boston Globe*, Dr. Thomas Pettigrew of Harvard, George Thomas of the Harvard School of Education, Lawrence O'Connell of Syracuse University, and many other individuals and organizations who supplied valuable assistance and, often, a great deal of hospitality. Horace W. Hewlett, Secretary of Amherst College and my associate for eleven years, always cheerfully encouraged my work and helped me to find the time to do it. Finally I must express my gratitude to Mrs. Linda Cail who converted illegible scribbles into a readable manuscript, and to Andrew and Mitzi Schrag, who helped prepare an index in record time.

CONTENTS

VILLAGE SCHOOL DOWNTOWN

PUBLIC EDUCATION in America has become education in—and for—metropolitan areas. Two of every three American children attend school in a city or a nearby suburb and approximately one in ten is educated in one of the twenty largest central cities: New York, Chicago, Los Angeles, Philadelphia, Detroit, Baltimore, Houston, Cleveland, St. Louis, Milwaukee, San Francisco, Boston, Dallas, New Orleans, Pittsburgh, San Diego, Seattle, Denver, Atlanta, Indianapolis. Among the children of minorities and among the disadvantaged, the proportion is even greater. New York City alone educates more children than Delaware, Montana, Nevada, New Hampshire, New Mexico, North Dakota, Rhode Island, Utah, and Vermont combined, and even a relatively small city like Boston runs a school establishment as large as that of the State of Idaho.

Because it operates at the very heart of contemporary political and social change, the urban school has the most crucial and difficult of educational responsibilities. The city is the locus of the new technology, the battleground of racial politics, the source of new expectations, and the shaper of the nation's cultural and ideological fashions. It is the city that defines the American style, that determines its economic and social behavior, and that generates its intellectual and moral complexity. To a great extent, therefore, American education has become urban education—not only in numbers, but presumably in content and in substance. And to an even greater extent the burden of the urban future is the burden of the urban school. For almost a decade the focus of northern civil rights pres-

1

sure has been on the schools; for almost a generation the schools have been losing middle-class children and gaining disadvantaged Negroes, Appalachian mountaineers, Puerto Ricans, Mexican-Americans, Indians, West Indians, and others. The schools have been boycotted and picketed; they have been assaulted by reformers and reactionaries; and they have been increasingly abandoned by the people whose support they need most. Many of them are underfinanced and understaffed. They suffer from ancient plants, ancient practices, and rigid hierarchies which, despite the efforts of the reformers, change but slowly—if, indeed, they change at all. In the city, the center of all that is presumably modern and dynamic, public education often remains the sluggish legacy of another age.

This is the particular story of one of those cities—and the general story of them all. Clearly no single example is typical of every situation. Differing political traditions and social attitudes, the varying patterns of population, the whole spectrum of educational practice, political structure, legislative requirements, and public policy give each community distinctive characteristics and problems, and suggest distinctive strategies to confront them. What may be appropriate in New York is ineffective in Houston; the things that seem to be problems in San Francisco may not yet be—or may never be—problems in Pittsburgh. And yet, despite the differences, there are common problems and a common set of consequences in education and social policy. All cities have problems of *de facto* segregation; they all seem to change slowly—are slow to abandon traditional practices; they all confront similar shortages of resources; and they all suffer from the white flight to the periphery and from the competition of suburban systems.

The questions one asks in Boston are the same questions one can ask in Chicago or New York or San Francisco, and they inevitably involve the same language: segregation, deprivation, neighborhood schools, busing, compensatory education, tracking, employment, housing, renewal, middle-class attitudes, process-centered learning, Title I, state aid, civil rights. What are the schools really about? Are they concerned with ritual, routine, and order, or are they genuinely committed to the development of intellectual skills, to nurturing curiosity, and toward producing genuinely independent human beings? What forces and attitudes have produced and maintained these schools, and how are these attitudes reflected in the classroom? What is the relationship between the political and social structure of the community and the educational program of the system, and how does one shape the other? Where are the sources of new ideas, and where the elements of the *status quo?* What does the community really expect of the schools? What do the civil rights groups want? And what do the lower-middle-class whites want? Are they genuinely interested in quality education, or do they regard the schools as bastions of discipline and character, and as fortresses that command the valleys of ethnic change? Will they accept integration, and if so, how much? In what respects have urban schools effectively responded to social and technological change— that is, in what way are urban schools genuinely urban at all, and in what way are they merely rural schools located in the city? What is the relation between education downtown and education in the periphery? Can city schools really take advantage of the city? To what extent can genuinely outstanding education contribute to a solution of other urban problems—to say nothing of alleviating the human misery from which they grow? Such questions are an integral part of the rhetoric and consciousness of our time; they underlie our changing awareness of what urban life in the last third of the twentieth century is about. In the midst of our culture stands the city. In the midst of the city stands the school.

Boston is probably no more or less typical of the situation of urban education than any other metropolis. It has unique characteristics, and it is subject to some relatively distinct political limitations. At the same time its elected school committee and its well-publicized political and educational battles make it an ideal place to examine what it is that the community presumably wants from its public schools. In Chicago or San Francisco it may be possible to charge that the mayor-appointed school boards do not faithfully reflect the wishes of the electorate. In Boston, for better or worse, all school issues are political issues subject to the electoral process. Everything in Boston is visible (to the extent that public decisions are ever visible); everything is political. Because Boston's school policies are subject to electoral review every two years, and because of the personalities and problems that the city's politics and social attitudes have thrown into public view, the city has become a center of national attention. The activities of the School Committee and of Mrs. Louise Day Hicks, its most prominent member, the city's unyielding intransigence in admitting that *de facto* segregation even exists, the city's boycotts, and its racial and educational policies have all given it a barometer quality that other communities have watched. One cannot fairly say that as Boston goes, so goes the nation; yet it is clear that whatever Boston does will be loud, visible, and colorful.

But the particular problems of one city are, in many respects, merely manifestations of controversies and difficulties that beset them all. Thus, while this book is focused on Boston, its concern is with urban education everywhere. The distinct and different situations of New York or San Francisco or Chicago are linked by common attitudes and produce common educational practices and similar sets of results. The schools of Evanston and Winnetka have much more in common with those of Scarsdale or Newton than they do with those of Chicago; education in Boston's Roxbury is distinct, but it resembles Harlem or the south side of Chicago far more than it does suburban Wellesley. And where there are common problems, there are also common solutions, or at least common ways of confronting the difficulties. The demands and opportunities of the economy and the technology observe no local boundaries; the social and moral complexities of the time honor no local traditions. Every school educates children for a national culture and a national economy; learning in Chicago must now also be learning for Detroit and New York. The local system can no longer be geared primarily to the local community.

* * *

The material in this book is based on research conducted in Boston during the academic year 1965–66. It included visits to elementary and secondary schools and classes, and to meetings of the School Committee; to neighborhood churches and social centers; to the storefront offices of protest groups; and to the streets and homes of the people for whom the schools are run. There were interviews with students, teachers, and administrators, with present and former members of the School Committee, with clergymen and journalists, with social workers and politicians, with university professors, and with the leaders of the major—and of many minor —organizations concerned in one way or another with public education in the city. The material in the book also relies heavily on

4

published reports in the city's major newspapers, on the literature of the Citizens for the Boston Schools, on the records and reports of the Boston School Department, the Boston Redevelopment Authority, the Chamber of Commerce, the Massachusetts State Department of Education, the NAACP and other civil rights organizations, the political tracts of School Committee candidates, the city's Negro press, especially the *Bay State Banner*, the neighborhood newspapers, and on a five-foot shelf of miscellaneous letters, pamphlets, reports, and other literature issued occasionally or regularly about the schools of Boston and vicinity.

The book also draws on some of the material gathered in the course of research for my book *Voices in the Classroom* (especially notes on suburban Newton, Massachusetts, and on San Francisco and Chicago) and on a substantial body of literature, formal and not-so-formal, concerning other urban systems and problems.

The list above is not intended either to bolster the evidence of the book—or even to express my dependence on, and gratitude to, my sources. Rather it is included as an indication of the tremendous number of individuals and the substantial body of material concerned with public education in one city. It illustrates the importance of the enterprise, the magnitude of its problems, and the opportunities that—properly conducted—the schools of the city can provide.

SHE STANDS large and immobile before the cameras, a small smile on her round face, a redundant ribbon on her beige dress proclaiming "I am Louise Day Hicks."

At this moment, in this place, no one needs to be told who she is. Today she won her third election to the five-member Boston School Committee, an office that, by itself, sheds only limited glory, no pay, and only the most paltry political power. But in the past two years she has achieved a notoriety that transcends the petty ambitions and the political grandstanding that have historically been associated with the committee: she has become a force, a symbol, a specter. Louise Hicks, the committee's chairman for the past year, has become the North's leading representative of resistance to school desegregation, its outstanding defender of neighborhood schools, a person who answers questions about busing with a "never" as emphatic as that of Sheriff Jim Clark of Selma or Chief Bull Connor of Birmingham. Recently she acquired a police dog for protection against persons who have allegedly threatened her.

The date is November 2, 1965, and around her are the friends and South Boston neighbors, the members of the Louise Day Hicks Association, who have faithfully supported her, who feel that she alone really stands up to "them," that she protects their small Irish homes and their desperately white neighborhoods. The president of the association, a Boston lawyer named John King, pins a corsage on her shoulder. Somewhere in the crowd a band strikes up "Every Little Breeze Seems to Whisper Louise" and then, echoing another era and other campaigns, "Happy Days Are Here Again." Before her, as the cameramen take their pictures, rests a florid three-tier cake inscribed *Best of Luck 1966–67*, and beside her stands a morose-faced man who is clearly unhabituated to bright lights and photographers, her relatively obscure husband, John Hicks. It is he who needs the ribbon with the identifying inscription.

"This—tonight—is a vote of confidence. The people are speaking," she declares. "Sometimes we hear just a vocal minority, but tonight, through the democratic process, we are hearing the majority. I will never redistrict for the sake of rebalancing. If you redistrict you may destroy the neighborhood schools. This victory belongs to all the people who believe in excellence and the good quality of education. In behalf of our children, I thank you."

The majority has indeed spoken, but not in behalf of excellence. The turnout today—48 percent of the city's 300,000 registered voters—represents a new record for an off-year election, when only City Council and School Committee seats are at stake. (The mayor is elected quadrennially.) And two thirds of those who came to the polls cast ballots for Mrs. Hicks. They defeated the only incumbent, sympathetic to the demands of Boston's civil rights leaders or critical of the system, and replaced him with the otherwise unknown brother of a city councilman. They defeated a bright, energetic Negro social worker named Melvin King, and they defeated three other challengers supported by the reform-minded Citizens for the Boston Schools. Except for the beaten liberal, Arthur Gartland, they returned the other incumbents to office:

Thomas S. Eisenstadt, the Catholic son of a Jewish father and an Irish mother, a young lawyer regarded as a politically ambitious upstart.

William E. O'Connor, an ex-schoolteacher who follows the Hicks line, and who is himself a product of the political-ethnic hierarchy that runs the Boston system.

Joseph Lee, a maverick Yankee who has no political ambitions, but who uses his seat on the committee as a platform for ex cathedra declarations on everything from economic theory to the virtues of physical exercise.

7

Together these three, along with Louise Day Hicks and the newcomer, John McDonough, are responsible for the operation of a school system comprising 93,000 children, 4,000 teachers and administrators, and 200 schools. In size it is roughly comparable to San Francisco or Denver or Milwaukee or Pittsburgh, but its problems—perhaps because of this School Committee—almost invariably appear larger, louder, and more dramatic. Boston's is the oldest public school system in the country. It is also among the most conservative, the most troubled, the most inbred. It suffers from all the difficulties plaguing most other American cities, as well as a few uniquely its own. Most emphatically it suffers from the absence of the middle-class families who have gone to the suburbs, from fragmented political authority, from the endless political quibbling of the School Committee, and from the political and ethnic traditions of the Irish politicians and civil servants who have dominated Boston for more than half a century. Although the tradition of the Curleys and the Honey Fitzes has begun to fade in general Boston city politics, the School Committee and the bureaucrats that administer the system still faithfully reflect the old style, the old habits, the old beliefs.

Mrs. Hicks is not a fluke, an accident of the electoral process. She is what Boston wants, and now—having just completed one campaign—she has become so important that she is being mentioned as a possible candidate for mayor, as the putative leader of a national campaign against school integration, and as America's foremost crusader for neighborhood schools. Joseph Alsop, the columnist, comes to Boston and calls her a potential Joe McCarthy dressed as Pollyanna, another reporter calls her a monster created by the newspapers, while a lot of people simply call her a bigot. But they do not represent the majority of the city's 620,000 residents—the Irish, the Italians, and, increasingly, the Lithuanians who are moving in among the Irish of South Boston. They do not represent the majority of the Boston teachers, the custodians, the nurses, and the other employees of the system, or the policemen and firemen whom Louise considers among her most loyal adherents, or the minor civil servants, the clerks and stevedores, the truck drivers and saloon keepers and real estate operators, or the middle-aged housewives of South Boston, Dorchester, and Charlestown, all of whom fear the small but growing Negro minority

8

and who lack the inclination or the resources to jump across the confining city limits. Approximately 12 percent of Boston's population is colored, one of the smallest concentrations in any major American city: New York is 14 precent Negro, Chicago 23 percent, Philadelphia 26 percent, Pittsburgh 17 percent, Washington 53 percent. But the Negro minority, which had never before been vocal, has suddenly become militant and has begun to generate resentment and fear among the poorer whites of the city who had traditionally looked down on their colored brothers with an abstract and passive tolerance.

Election day in 1965 brought an unequivocal vote for "the neighborhood school" and whatever that idea suggested in the minds of the electorate. It was not a casual campaign, or one in which the issues became obscured. The slate supported by the Citizens for the Boston Schools—liberal incumbent Arthur Gartland, the Negro social worker Melvin King, and the three others—campaigned hard, with what proved to be suicidal effectiveness. There had been rallies and parades, bands and speeches, motorcades and sound trucks, television panels, and, night after night, the small gatherings, the kaffee klatsches, the endless meetings in church basements and school auditoriums.

Two days before the election there is a parade through the Negro ghetto of Roxbury—a white Catholic school band, a convertible with six attractive Negro girls wearing yellow caps labelled King Kadets, children, friends of the candidate, and a group of white South End intellectuals wearing paper hats labelled King. Inside the King headquarters, where the parade ends, there is a rock 'n' roll band, hundreds of kids, and noise, and coffee, and smoke. King and some of the other Citizen candidates go through the crowd shaking hands: "I want you to go out there Tuesday and vote . . ." A Radcliffe College girl is passing out sheets with the lyrics of civil rights songs and special campaign verses. A few people sing—to the tune of "When Johnny Comes Marching Home":

> For freedom to come to Roxbury
> Come out, come out,
> We need a better school committee
> So come out, come out . . .

But the rock 'n' roll band and the general chatter finally overcome. "We can win this election if . . ."

> . . . A new committee is our only way
> So come out and vote on our election day . . .

Then more noise as they cheer King's words at the microphone, applause, spilled coffee, kids, and the candidate is off, this time to a South End gathering with canapes and Scotch.

In the month preceding the election—as Mrs. Hicks met with small groups in homes and social clubs all through the middle- and lower-middle-class neighborhoods of Hyde Park and Dorchester and Jamaica Plain—the Citizens sent out a stream of releases and statements, and assembled an organization that tried its best to be practical, political, and efficient. A considerable amount of money was raised, the Junior Chamber of Commerce voiced support and provided some manpower and helped nourish the hope that, as one of the reform leaders said, "Boston has woken up a little bit." Mayor Collins—it was said—had agreed "not to let his people knife us." (Neither will he support the challengers; only one Boston voter in ten is Negro.) But the Citizens' organization—young lawyers, League of Women Voters ladies, social workers, academics—most of them persons more interested in municipal improvement and abstract political morality than in personal friendships and power—never made the impact it hoped.

Normally in the biennial Boston School Committee elections, every man runs for himself; a September primary eliminates all but ten candidates, each of whom hopes to be one of the five chosen by the electorate in November. The campaigns are conducted by independent candidates, are frankly political, and rarely deal very much in educational issues. There is a myth in Boston that the School Committee is a stepping stone to higher office; in fact very few people ever manage to use it that way. Yet in a city where politics has always been a major step on the ladder to success, every preliminary School Committee election draws eighteen or twenty candidates, each expecting to get some public attention, some prestige, and ultimately—perhaps—a chance at higher office. For some it is a way of life. But since the campaigns are tough, expensive, and sometimes dirty, few outstanding individuals ever run. In 1965 the Citizens departed from their traditional pattern by endorsing not one or two, but five candidates who ran as a slate: Gartland, King, two well-meaning but undynamic Irish Catholics, and an Italian Catholic lady who works for a State employment agency. They thus saddled Gartland with three weak running mates (the best that were available), deprived him of his advantage as an incumbent, and made him, psychologically, an outside challenger. At the same time their strategy helped pin the unknown John McDonough to the tails of the incumbent majority—Mrs. Hicks and O'Connor both endorsed him—and converted the campaign into a partisan election in which one side had a powerful emotional issue while the other was able to deal only in educational matters of limited popular appeal.

The Citizen candidates spoke about how the schools, especially in the Negro areas of the South End and Roxbury, were overcrowded and antiquated, about the many temporary teachers, about Boston's poor performance in the percentage of students going on to college, about its archaic vocational programs, about inbreeding and budgetary inefficiency. They spoke about inequities between white and Negro schools, about Boston's unbelievable failure to construct new buildings—even though the money was theoretically available—and, again and again, about its general conservatism. But these issues seemed to matter little to the voters. "It's pretty hard to impress the parents of parochial school children with the problem of overcrowding," said a South Boston father, "when their own kids are crammed into classrooms with fifty or sixty others." One of the candidates pointed out that "some of the parish priests may be for good schools and against segregation, but when they keep telling their own people that it's all right to have big classes—that the nuns can handle them fine—then they're helping Louise, not us." When Gartland spoke about high teacher turnover, or about the sloppy handling of the budget, Mrs. Hicks shot back remarks about "our dedicated teachers," voted to raise custodians' salaries, and got herself photographed with the officers of the Custodians Association which, not surprisingly, had endorsed her. "You can't make an impact on this town," Mel King, the Negro candidate, said later. "If you speak about kids not getting into college they tell you the Superintendent says we're doing fine, and whenever you criticize the schools you run into the old problem: Everybody has a brother or a cousin who works for the School Department, and they all think the schools are wonderful."

The issue that became clear, and the only issue, was that of busing and neighborhood schools; and it came into focus almost independently of the campaign itself. In the summer of 1965, before anyone had begun thinking seriously about the election, Superintendent William H. Ohrenberger innocently recommended that the city bus several hundred children from overcrowded Negro schools to underutilized—and incidentally white—schools. The School Committee—inspired not by Mrs. Hicks, but by Eisenstadt—rejected the recommendation as contrary to policy, even though busing had been used to relieve overcrowding in Boston before. (Eisenstadt later explained that his reasons for opposing Ohrenberger's plan were based on budgetary considerations and on a feeling that the administration—which, he said, had already contracted for the buses—was usurping the School Committee's prerogatives. But that explanation came long after the election, and after Eisenstadt had begun to adopt a more moderate position. At the time, he managed to cash in on a political issue that Mrs. Hicks had previously monopolized in the public mind.) For weeks thereafter the committee argued about double sessions, about buying a discarded Hebrew school (Roxbury, once Jewish, is littered with old synagogues), and about setting up what Boston calls "demountable classrooms." Mrs. Hicks urged that the committee give priority to the construction of a new school in the overcrowded district, a recommendation that prompted the Citizens to declare "that since even Mrs. Hicks knows it takes at least four years to build a school in Boston, this hardly qualifies as 'speedy.' " Concurrently Boston Mayor John F. Collins, who, by virtue of a constitutional division of power, has a major voice in all school construction and building acquisitions, vetoed the Hebrew school as inadequate. Portable classrooms could not be set up for several months, and, as the opening of school became imminent, only double sessions in the affected Negro schools remained as a possibility. As a final measure, Ohrenberger requested that the Committee rescind its now-futile order to buy the Hebrew school and thereby free the appropriated funds for other purposes; the request was denied, despite the mounting criticism of the Citizens, the Negro community, and the *Boston Globe*. No one outside of Roxbury appeared very much concerned.

Late in August—with the first day of school only two weeks off—a group of Negro parents, led by Mrs. Ellen Jackson and Mrs. Betty Johnson, both Roxbury area residents, took independent steps. Acting under an open enrollment policy which permits children to attend any school not already filled, they organized their own busing program, Operation Exodus. At a cost of $1,200 a week, most of it raised in the slums or the outlying suburbs, at charity dances, and in mothers' marches, the Exodus parents began to transport several hundred children out of the ghetto.

And as Exodus got under way early in September, so did the School Committee election campaign, and one colored the other. The Negro mothers moved into a store on Blue Hill Avenue, Main Street of Negro Roxbury, and began to raise funds (they are still doing it), to direct their fleet of chartered buses, and to conduct an after-school tutoring program. It turned out to be one of the most magnificently organized and operated programs ever conducted in a northern slum, even though it committed resources badly needed for other forms of protest and social action. Each day 300 children were picked up at the Blue Hill address and elsewhere and hauled far into white neighborhoods where, the mothers said, the schools were better, the teachers superior, and the books more relevant, and where, they felt, their children were being treated more sympathetically than they had been in the slums. But no sooner had they started their program than Mrs. Hicks, followed by reporters, showed up at one of the receiving schools to remind the children that they needed their "yellow slips," required for transfer under open enrollment. It was a small gesture but it established, for the rest of the campaign, a counterpoint between her presence and the reality of busing, of transporting Negro children into white schools. (Later she called the whole program "Operation Disruption.")

The Citizens' candidates insisted that the race issue helped Mrs. Hicks and the other incumbents hide the genuine educational failures of the system, but they were unable themselves to get away from it. In the first place, of course, it was simply a fact that there was a race issue, that for the past two years the

NAACP and other civil rights organizations had dramatized it, that there had been boycotts and petitions and marches, and that the School Committee had refused even to give official recognition to the matter of *de facto* segregation. For several months in the spring of 1965 a Negro minister named Vernon Carter had maintained a one-man picket line at School Committee headquarters, pledging to continue his vigil until either the state or the schools acted to recognize the problem. Living in a trailer near the School Committee headquarters, and handing picket signs to any passerby who would carry one, Carter helped dramatize the race issue in Boston and to spur passage through the legislature (just a few steps down Beacon Street from the School Committee) of what became the nation's first state law against *de facto* segregation in the public schools. (The Massachusetts Racial Imbalance Law requires communities to take steps to eliminate racial imbalance in the schools and to arrange attendance districts and new construction to minimize it, and it authorizes the State Department of Education to withhold funds from those school systems that have not adopted acceptable plans of compliance.)

More important, the incumbents themselves—excluding only Lee, who didn't campaign at all, and Arthur Gartland—kept the race issue alive, going about the city making dire predictions about busing. Committeeman William E. O'Connor, who, if anything, was even more adamant than Louise Hicks, asserted that "there is no guarantee that racially balancing the schools will improve the Negroes' learning ability. Often the Negro child and parent are not doing their job. . . ." The Citizens, he warned, "presently are for busing in only one direction, all that is allowed under the state law, but I predict that within a year they will be working to have the law permit compulsory two-way busing of pupils as the only way to get racial balance in Boston's schools." The Citizens' organization retorted that O'Connor "should put down his Halloween pumpkin and let the electorate look at his record. He is desperately trying to panic the voters. The Citizens don't ask pledges about busing or anything else from their candidates." One of the Citizens' candidates accused O'Connor of bigotry, calling him a "pious fraud pulling every dirty trick in the book in an effort to save his skin." But the tactic, if that is what it was, worked.

And O'Connor was not the only incumbent to use it, although he used it most blatantly. Louise Hicks said again and again that she would never bus children to achieve racial balance, that children should stay in their own neighborhoods where they could go to school with their friends and playmates, that she feared the cultural shock busing might produce. "People around here are afraid of Negroes," said a South Boston Irish father. "There is no crime, no rapes. They think Mrs. Hicks is keeping them out." That statement accurately reflected a prevailing set of white fears— fears common to the lower-middle-class of many cities, who, if they have nothing else, can at least boast of their respectability. (Boston has had a fairly moderate crime rate; shortly after the election, however, it suffered a vicious wave of violent crimes, many of them committed by whites in Irish South Boston. Beginning in the spring of 1966, there were daily reports of looting, theft, murder, and malicious destruction of property in the very precincts that mythology portrayed as being so peaceful and harmonious. But that was after the election; probably, moreover, it would not have affected the outcome even if it had started before. Crime meant Negroes, and rape—given the Irish fear of sex— meant Negroes at their very worst.)

As the campaign entered its final weeks—and as Exodus continued, with plenty of local publicity—the imbalance controversy received more and more attention while the blurry educational issues (and there was no evidence that the voters were ever seriously interested in educational quality) almost vanished from public debate. "All they ask me," said one of the Citizen candidates, "is 'are you for busing?' and 'are you for Mrs. Hicks?' " There was talk about an impending federal investigation of segregation in the Boston schools—never heard from again—and repeated threats that Boston would lose State aid under the imbalance law, or federal aid under the Civil Rights Act of 1964 if racial imbalance were not eliminated. (The critics took heart when Francis Keppel, then U.S. Commissioner of Education, acted as if he might withhold funds from Chicago; when Lyndon Johnson overruled Keppel—and when it became clear that Washington had no intention of applying the Civil Rights Act to de facto segregation —the federal argument vanished from the Boston campaign.) Mrs. Hicks, responding to the warnings with words vaguely reminiscent of the rhetoric of the redneck, declared that if funds were withheld "they'll hear from me," and intimated that if it came to a showdown she would rather lose the money than balance the schools. She and O'Connor, acting through a friendly member of the state legislature, had already filed a bill to repeal the imbalance law.

While these exchanges took place, there came an uninterrupted stream of civil rights pronouncements from civic leaders, manifestoes from groups of clergymen, and even editorials in *The Pilot*, the official organ of the Boston Catholic archdiocese. Richard Cardinal Cushing, who heads the archdiocese, and who is probably the most prominent man in Boston, had been a member of the Kiernan Commission which had described, and sharply condemned, *de facto* segregation in the city; it was the Kiernan Report, signed by Cushing and many other prominent Massachusetts citizens, that formed the basis of the imbalance law. The clerical declarations and the civic statements and pronouncements rang with indignation at the intransigence of the incumbent School Committee majority—representing them as violators of the law, as morally deficient, as betrayers of little children, and they kept the race issue in the foreground. But they persuaded no one. Cushing's attitude—which was apparently clear to Boston's overwhelmingly Catholic population (about 80 percent)—had little effect. (In one church the parish priest introduced one of the Cardinal's circular letters with a specific personal disclaimer, announcing it with the statement that "I have to read this." One of his liberal parishioners exclaimed that "that was the closest I ever came to hitting a priest.") Indeed, nothing seemed to have much effect, except to reiterate, again and again, the issue of racial imbalance. At the last, busing and the neighborhood school overwhelmed even the challengers. Toward the end of the campaign, the Citizens, apparently sensing how things were going, issued a flier stating:

Do you want your children bused?
NO! Neither do we!
The need for busing can be eliminated by building new schools.
We want to build new schools.

By the morning of November 2 there was not a shadow of a

doubt that Louise Hicks would win handily, and that most of the challengers would lose. The hope of the liberals was that King, the Negro, might displace O'Connor, the Irish ex-schoolteacher, thus giving Gartland an ally and reducing the Hicks margin on the Committee to 3–2 (or even possibly 2–2, since Yankee Joseph Lee could not be placed in any camp). But few people expected Gartland to be defeated, and it was that development that seemed to turn the election into a disaster and Louise Hicks into a giant. The winners carried all the Irish and Italian wards in Charlestown and South Boston, East Boston and Dorchester; they carried a substantial number of precincts in the middle-class areas, and they lost only the upper-middle-class Back Bay (composed largely of people with no personal stake in the schools) and the Negro districts in North Dorchester, Roxbury, and the South End where, in some wards, almost 90 percent of the registered voters turned out to support Gartland and King. City-wide, the election was a rout, with Louise Hicks gaining 92,000 votes while her nearest opponent had barely 50,000.

The returns placed the Boston System on a collision course with the imbalance law, and it started talk among Negro leaders about possibly seceding from the city school system altogether. (A few months later $4 million in state funds was withheld pending submission of an acceptable plan of compliance with the imbalance law. Concurrently several ghetto groups began discussing plans for establishing independent "public" schools with private or federal financing.) At his unhappy election headquarters in a Roxbury storefront, Mel King simply remarked, "A little bit of democracy died in Boston today." A few days later one of his financial backers and friends wrote him: "If the good guys work hard and dig up money and put everything they have into an election and the bad guys win time after time it is easy to say the hell with it and that the only approach which gets results is to throw bricks through the windows. One reason I hoped so strongly you'd win this time was that if a tough honest man won it would convince a lot of people that two and two actually did make four and that the world was a rational place and they might as well participate rationally in it. Which didn't work out. With the moral being that ignorance, fear, and prejudice remain the foundation of most people's political action. . . ." And elsewhere across the nation the

Boston returns cast a shadow over the prospects for desegregated schools: they were interpreted as sheer bigotry, as backlash, as the putrid effluent of white urban prejudice and fear, and as a grim portent for other cities. But at the Boston Club, where Louise Hicks and her friends were celebrating, the band struck up "Happy Days Are Here Again." On this particular night Louise Day Hicks seemed to have won all the marbles.

* * *

What makes this large, plain woman so successful? She is in her late forties, a practicing lawyer, mother of two sons, and—most significantly—the daughter of a South Boston Irish judge who had been just important enough to get a boulevard named after him. Because of her father, Judge William Day, she always calls herself Louise Day Hicks, never Mrs. John Hicks. In certain respects she is a shy woman—someone remarked that behind that rather chilly, uncomfortable facade lurks a little girl—a daughter of the lace curtain Irish who was never too proud to maintain childhood friendships, who did not move into the suburbs (she is convinced that busing would bring an accelerating exodus of whites), and who built a reputation as a person who remained loyal to the little people. As she speaks to the visitor in her office in the School Department building, three floors above the traffic on Beacon Street, she looks rather like a displaced clubwoman who hardly belongs in the public controversies that swirl about her: she is the perpetual innocent. Her father's last words, she says by way of justifying her own career, were to "look after them" —the little people, that is. "My father was a friend to them all. Your problems were his problems." In her reflections about the past and the present there is a strong sense of place—and the place, of course, is South Boston—as well as a powerful identification with Judge Day (he died in 1950), a man who knew everyone in his district and who, according to Mrs. Hicks, was once offered a federal judgeship by Calvin Coolidge (despite their differing political affiliations).

In 1961, running as a reform candidate pledged to keep school affairs out of politics, Mrs. Hicks won her first race for the School Committee. Her victory, one element of a general upset of a particularly odious School Committee majority, was based in part on a campaign to restore the Boston Latin School, the pride of the system, to its former glory, and partly on the strength of her many friends and associates in South Boston. There was no race issue, no talk of imbalance. Most people in Boston—certainly the Irish—took the Negro ghetto for granted. Toward the end of her first term Mrs. Hicks began to take a friendly and somewhat condescending interest in the education of the city's Negroes, but her early sympathetic flirtations with the Negro leadership foundered after her own ethnic and political conservatism began to collide with the increasing militancy of the NAACP.

In the spring of 1963, as the Boston civil rights leadership, sensing the winds of change, began to assert itself, Louise Hicks began to draw back. Already identifying with the little people of South Boston, she had also become a defender of the *status quo* at the School Department. When the NAACP equated Boston with Mississippi, and when it began to issue demands (no one in Boston had ever heard of a Negro organization demanding anything), she started to develop her reputation. That summer, serving as committee chairman, she stared down her first civil rights protests, brought out the first pickets, and identified herself as the budding symbol of northern intransigence toward civil rights demands. At the same time she won herself a reputation as a courageous woman, not only among the people that she calls "the people" but also among some Brahmin bankers and real estate dealers who are otherwise embarrassed by her. "Although I'm diametrically opposed to Mrs. Hicks," said Ralph Lowell, the board president of the New England Safe Deposit Company, "I think she's a courageous woman who's standing up for the things she believes in. That kind of courage has its appeal."

After the first confrontations, she took on not only the NAACP, but also the Congress of Racial Equality, the Mayor of Boston, various organizations of clergymen, Senator Edward Kennedy, Martin Luther King, the Cardinal, the State Board of Education, the legislature, and the federal courts. That became her style. She was threatened with violence and dramatically took out a weapons permit and acquired her dog, was the cause of repeated picketing and of two school boycotts, became the subject of puns ("Boston is a Hicks town") and of a great deal of newsroom innuendo. But she got the attention. In 1963 she led all candidates on the ballot, including the successful mayor, John F. Collins; and by 1965 she announced that she would be disappointed if she didn't lead the ticket again. She thus made *herself* an issue, operating squarely in the rambunctious Boston tradition, resisting the whole establishment on behalf of small people who never expect to make it big. (In his day, Mayor Curley took on President Roosevelt, the courts, the legislature, the Boston bluestockings, a different Cardinal, and a whole host of reformers gathered together as the Good Government Association and simply called—by Curley—the Goo-goos.) Although the Citizens for the Boston Schools—especially in the 1965 campaign—attracted people from all sorts of backgrounds, they still suffered from a Beacon Hill upper-class taint, were still identified more with Harvard, the banks, and Yankeedom than with South Boston and the working man. Thus when Mrs. Hicks' neighbors in Ward 7 spoke that fall about "standing up to *them*"—and many did—they seemed to be thinking not only of the Negro civil rights leaders, but also of all the other unnamed, nebulous devils associated with corporate exploitation, upper-class snobbery, and suburban hypocrisy. For more than forty years the respectable and well-heeled had neglected the inner city and its slums, had excluded the new immigrants, had posted signs that "no Irish need apply." Now they were in effect telling the Irish and the Italians to atone for their old sins and balance the schools. And Louise Day Hicks, sensing the fear, and the injustice, was telling them all to go to hell.

Louise Hicks shudders that, in 1965, she might have received the votes of some bigots. She is proud of her achievements on behalf of "our children" (*her* children, as she did, herself, attended parochial schools), pleased at the schools' growing program of compensatory education for deprived youngsters, and by a number of other educational improvements that she feels she helped foster. But she acknowledges what others have long said: it was the imbalance issue—neighborhood schools—not educational considerations that decided the outcome. The greatest difference between those who voted for her and those who voted against her, according to a survey conducted by Prof. Thomas Pettigrew of Harvard, was in home ownership and residential stability. Her supporters were people who owned small homes, and who have lived at the same address for better than ten years. Her opponents tended much more to be renters, to be mobile, and to be even less committed to the public schools than her supporters. According to Pettigrew, 75 percent of the people who voted for her do not have, or even expect to have, children in the public schools; but 90 percent of those who voted *against* her are in the same category. Boston is a city of old people. The survey found that her supporters included a higher proportion of people with strong prejudices and authoritarian attitudes—that is, more bigots—than her opponents; but it also indicated that most people who voted for her saw her as more anti-Negro than they saw themselves. "She made respectable in the public media," someone said, "things that were usually expressed only in barrooms and street corners." On the whole, Mrs. Hicks received the vote of the lower-middle-class Irish, the Italians, and other groups, while most Jews—and, of course, the Negroes—voted against her. As soon as the returns were known she began to receive fan mail from every part of the country ("your smashing victory echoed through the mountains"), and, a few days later, she trooped off to California where, it was said, she was to be installed as the grand national leader of a neighborhood school crusade. (Somehow that movement, too, has faded into the recesses of memory.) There were letters and telegrams, to go along with such things as a commendation from a Polish-American anti-Communist organization, and the outstanding citizen citation for 1965 of the South Boston Citizens Association. Earlier in the year Massachusetts Senator Edward M. Kennedy had publicly criticized *de facto* segregation in the Boston schools. "He would have been shocked at the mail," she said shortly after the 1965 election. "He would have been shocked."

And yet to say that bigotry, the fear of Negroes, or some pathological anxiety about real estate are the only factors in Mrs. Hicks' success would be to indicate that any individual appealing to prejudice could have been done as much. It would deny the tremendous image that she has generated about herself. Her constant references to "our children" and "our dedicated teachers," her apparently genuine concern that certain classroom teachers not get lost in bureaucratic shuffles, her role as the protectress—of children, of teachers, of neighborhoods—all of these things have helped to shape this political Kate Smith. She has become Boston's head mother.

The image is important and entirely consistent with the Boston school system as an educational and social establishment, and with the history of the city itself. In other places Louise Day Hicks would simply be some curbstone spokesman for a Parents and Tax-payers Committee, carrying a placard protesting the busing that a conservative, but more reasonable school committee was incapable of doing anyway. "If we had Calvin Gross (the one-time New York City superintendent) here in Boston," said Mrs. Ruth Bat-son, the former education chairman of the NAACP, "we'd be in ecstasy. In New York they kicked him around." It is not simply that Louise Day Hicks is more rigid, or perhaps less suave, it is that she perfectly reflects the negative aspirations of a school sys-tem as conservative and hierarchical as any in the nation. "She ad-vocates the neighborhood school system," said a South Boston woman, "and what's wrong with that? When I was a kid we all went to schools in our neighborhood. Once I wanted to transfer from the old school in our neighborhood to a brand new school they'd built called the Jeremiah Burke. But I lived on the wrong side of Bloomfield Avenue and I had to stay where I was. If I could live with it, why can't the people in Roxbury? And all this talk about overcrowded classrooms. All these civil rights people think thirty-five people are too many for one room. It's all a matter of discipline. You don't see any of the kids in the parochial schools talking back to the nuns." Boston's schools operate alongside a parochial system that enrolls 40,000 students (about one third of the city's children), that has educated a good many of its public school teachers, and that in its devotion to discipline, hierarchy, and authority has deeply influenced the public system over the years. In such a situation Mrs. Hicks can be not only the defender of the neighborhood, she can also be the enforcer of order and dis-cipline, wise, courageous, and firm. Not only the head mother, but also the mother superior. She keeps the faith.

Because she is a woman, and because she is the woman she is, it is unlikely that she will ever succeed in achieving higher of-fice. A majority of the people who voted for her in 1965 would not vote for her for mayor, according to the Pettigrew survey, a con-clusion that led someone to observe that in the man's world of city hall the image of the great mother would turn into the nag-ging wife. But it is also clear that much of Mrs. Hicks' support comes from people who are confused and frightened by the pace of social change, who share the Goldwater view that "we feel adrift in an uncharted land and stormy sea. We feel we have lost our way." Her votes came from people trapped between their conservatism and their dependency on the welfare state, and who, in times of social stress, seem rapidly to multiply in the body politic. Shortly after the election there was a typical Boston rumor that "the Kennedys" were trying to check the political career of this South Boston upstart, that they were fearful of her obvious appeal to the northern bigots; Mrs. Hicks, so the rumor went, had the support of the McCormack faction, which was trying to embarrass the Kennedys. House Speaker John McCormack had been a close friend of Judge Day, Mrs. Hicks' father, and he still lives just a few blocks from Mrs. Hicks on Columbia Road. McCormack's nephew Edward had run against Teddy Kennedy for the Democratic senatorial nomination; Teddy had criticized Mrs. Hicks and the School Committee, the McCormacks had not. These elements represented just another example of Boston's favorite pastime—the manufacture and dissemination of good political tales. But the rumors also illustrated how large Mrs. Hicks appeared after the election of November 2, and how significant were its results.

IN THE BOSTON of Mayors James Michael Curley and John F. "Honey Fitz" Fitzgerald, the Cabots spoke only to the Lowells but the Irish ran the city. Sometimes they ran it from a West End ward or, like Curley, from a federal prison, but one way or another, they ran it. And still run it.

Styles, of course, have changed. Mayor John F. Collins, who has served the city with energy since 1959, is known as a Chamber of Commerce Irishman; and Arthur Gartland—in two terms on the School Committee—was known as a Harvard Irishman. In the "New" Boston of the sixties, boasting urban progress and redevelopment, any citizen will speak to almost any other, honored political habits are breaking down, and even Scollay Square—the boozy honky-tonk of all-night bars, burlesque houses, and other delights of the flesh—has been razed by the renewers. Not even the old subway station sign remains to indicate where the Square used to be. Yet, characteristically, the project which replaced Scollay—the Government Center, one of the two most ambitious renewal projects ever undertaken in Boston—is almost entirely devoted to the storage of that most typical of Bostonians, the civil servant. Of the 288,000 people employed in the city, 24,000 (one of every twelve) are listed as public administrators and another 14,000 are associated with educational or medical enterprises. (In San Francisco, with 331,000 in the working force, one in fifteen is a public employee; in Chicago one in twenty; in Pittsburgh, one in nineteen.) But it is not the number or the concentration that makes the difference—Boston, after all, is a state capital—but the attitude. Because other jobs were closed to them, or not available at all, the new immigrants, and especially the Irish, gravitated toward politics and public employment. Nowhere else in America has civil service, its limited opportunities, its structure, and its pace, so dominated the general outlook. In the John F. Kennedy Federal Center, and in a new city hall, resembling some sort of Sumerian temple, both going up in close proximity to an already existing state office building, there will be tiers upon tiers of bureaucrats, functionaries, and officials. (Every day, as the Government Center—perhaps the prime symbol of redevelopment in Boston—was rising to its sterile heights, the old Scollay Square rummies wandered aimlessly through the area, like the survivors of a thriving anthill destroyed by an arrogant foot. Ultimately perhaps, the history of contemporary America will be seen as the replacement of the bum by the bureaucrat.)

Despite the monstrosity of the Government Center, however—some say because of it—the city has now apparently ended more than thirty years of stagnation and two decades of population decline (from 800,000 in 1950 to 620,000 in 1965). There is a new tone, and a new urban optimism, best personified, perhaps, by the city's dynamic, tough-talking urban renewal administrator, Edward J. Logue. To Logue "what is happening in Boston right now is the most exciting thing in the world." A thoroughly political man—none other could survive in Boston—Logue is responsible for making the city think big for the first time in recent history. With the support of Mayor Collins, who brought Logue to Boston in 1960, he has banged conservative heads, promoted ambitious plans, and battled Yankee bankers and Irish pols with equal enthusiasm. In the process he has secured some $150 million in federal funds for redevelopment and has begun to change the face of the city. "I don't believe in being neutral," he said during a scrap a few years ago. "And I believe in fighting to win. I won't sit back, as some of my colleagues in renewal do, and let my political support go down the drain." If redevelopment under Logue continually runs into political battles and into charges of administrative brutality, it can still be said that the old Brahmins, the moguls of the Chamber of Commerce, and the city politicians have—for better or worse—started to work together, something they haven't done since the beginning of this century. But the problems, nonetheless, remain staggering.

Boston is every American's Great Historic Site, the city of the Massacre and the Tea Party, of Sam Adams and Paul Revere, of Anne Hutchinson and John Cotton, of the Kennedys and McCormacks, and of all those proper people who once lived in the Back Bay and on Beacon Hill but who are now as plentiful in exurbs like Duxbury, Lincoln, and Beverly. Like many another American metropolis Boston has been savagely victimized by the flight of the middle class from the central city—although Beacon Hill is still *the* place to live—and it has had, until recently, almost no major new development since the depression. Its stagnant tax base reels under the burden of new services, as well as some of the lushest pension and welfare programs ever devised by man. Although many other cities are suffering from the suburbanization of commerce and industry, few have been hit as hard as Boston. In the fifties, while New York added major new office buildings to its tax rolls each year, Boston's total assessed valuation declined by half a billion dollars through depreciation or conversion to nontaxable uses, giving the city one of the highest effective tax rates in America. Boston, moreover, has been hemmed in by suburbs jealously guarding their legislative influence, and hobbled by fragmented political control. Three fourths of the 2,600,000 people in the metropolitan area do not live in the city (in New York, three fourths do live inside; in Milwaukee the ratio is six in ten), and they are reluctant to give the city any more political jurisdiction than it already has. Over the years, people fearful of the rising Irish city politicians have vested municipal powers in special metropolitan commissions and districts, or have placed it in the hands of the governor and legislature. Boston does not choose its own Finance Commission—which can scrutinize all city affairs—or regulate its own liquor sales, and it has only partial control over its transportation system, its water supply, and its parks. Concurrently the city has been constricted for more than a half century by a financial and social conservatism that preferred a safe five percent trust and a Friday seat at Symphony—rarely called the Boston Symphony—to anything that smacked too much of risk, adventure, or association with new groups. Thus when the Irish, Italians, and the other new immigrants arrived in the three generations after 1850, they found a city whose main avenues to advancement began with politics and civil service, not with corporate enterprise or industrial growth. Its median family income is now $5,700 (1960), one of the lowest among major American cities.

Boston literally missed the boat. Although the city's capitalists helped finance several transcontinental railroads they failed to develop one of their own, and thus Boston never became the great seaport that its geographical location might have made possible. The local conservatism—always aiming to keep family control of relatively small enterprises—ignored several major opportunities to bring heavy manufacturing industries to the city, directed the available capital to restrictive trust funds, and staffed the city's businesses—banks, real estate firms, insurance companies—with the not-always competent sons of proper families. Cleveland Amory, the chronicler of the foibles of proper Bostonians, tells the story of the Chicago banking firm that queried a Boston investment house about a young man being considered for employment. The reply enthusiastically affirmed that the man's father was a Cabot, his mother a Lowell, and that behind them was a blend of Saltonstalls, Peabodys, and Appletons, all members of Boston's first families. To which the Chicago employer replied with thanks, explaining that "we were not contemplating using [the gentleman] for breeding purposes."

Boston—the Hub—is preeminently the city of institutions. Institutions have given it its reputation and depleted it of its tax base, have occupied its talent and thereby—probably—weakened its politics. Two of the best known, Harvard and the Massachusetts Institute of Technology, are not in Boston at all, although Harvard has cast a shadow across the city three centuries long and several traditions broad. But not Harvard nor M.I.T. nor Boston University, nor the Massachusetts General Hospital, nor the Boston Symphony, not even the once powerful Watch and Ward Society, nor the still powerful Roman Catholic archdiocese, defines what makes the city so institutional. It is, of course, true that when Richard Cardinal Cushing visits Ireland or dedicates a school or delivers a pronouncement it is front-page news, that when a cantankerous Irishman seething with contempt for the Ivy League is invited to lunch at the Harvard Club he does not refuse, and that it is never supposed to rain on the day of a Harvard Commencement—and apparently never does. But these are peripheral matters. The central issue is simply that Boston is institution-minded, and that for the proper people all institutions are like the military or civil service in their structure and in their function of defining limits, success, and position. This institutional mentality, Boston's failure to develop economically, and its blueblood First Family conservatism have all reinforced each other, have had their effect on the development of the city, and have dramatically influenced the economic and cultural fortunes of the newer immigrants, particularly those of the Irish who flooded into the city through the latter half of the nineteenth century and well into the twentieth and who still dominate its public life. Boston often resembles a European city in its network of commercial and public sinecures, in its fixed classes and estates. While other American communities teemed with brash enterprise, there was a place in Boston for everyone who was already there, but the places were fixed: the scions of good families were brought into the banks, the textile firms, and the investment companies, were taught to manage the trusts, and learned to become directors of hospitals and welfare societies; the offspring of the poor were taken into the church, the police force, and the clerical jobs that the state and municipal governments provided, but they rarely got a chance to compete, except in ward politics. There were no new enterprises, and those that already existed were closed to outsiders. That Boston lady's remark—"Why should I travel when I'm already here?"—applied as well to financial and commercial odysseys as it did to more conventional journeys.

One of the reasons why the Boston Irish are so thoroughly committed to the institutions of the church and the military is that it became *their* Church, and that the Army, like the civil service, represented a place where the Paddies and Mikes were accepted on equal terms and where, given the proper circumstances, they could rise to places of honor and esteem. South Boston has treated pacifist demonstrations with more violence than almost any other place in America, probably because they threaten one of the few institutions where the Irish have been able to become one hundred percent Americans. Unlike the second generation Poles of Chicago or the Hungarians of Pittsburgh, their defensive hostility against the incursions and demands of Negroes is not based on the competitiveness of recent achievement, but rather on a view of the world in which everyone has a place, and in which all opportunities are limited. The Irish areas of South Boston and Dorchester are not territories that their upwardly mobile inhabitants recently captured; they are, rather, ancient tribal domains, institutions in their own right. They are artifacts of the city's institutional mind and relics of its restricted economic life.

Boston's limited perspective has been more than a century in the making. In 1911, when Arnold Bennett visited the city, he remarked that "What primarily differentiates Boston from all the other American cities is this: It is finished. I mean complete. Of the other cities, one would say 'They will be. Boston is.' " It is the sense of completion that has marked it for the past fifty years. William V. Shannon, a social historian of American Irish, has accurately described the process that formed the Boston mind, and that produced the city's economic and social stagnation:

> The dynamic Yankee businessman of the old era had begun to harden by the 1850's into the conservative Brahmin. By 1900 this class had retreated still further. The archetype of a once virile and creative ruling group became the Back Bay gentleman who reputedly reinvested his dividends and lived on the income from his income. The drop in quality from the elder Holmes to the late George Apley was a measure of the toll the past century had taken of the Boston aristocracy.
>
> While members of this *rentier* class occupied themselves with their sailboats and their genealogies, the managers of the economy moved crabwise. Men whose thinking was molded by their service in the banks and trust companies of State Street fumbled over the small decisions and tried to avoid the big ones. Caution, traditionally a watchword of the Boston financial district, was exalted into an even higher plane in its hierarchy of values. Much that was only vulgar—inertia, ignorance, economic nepotism—masqueraded as high-minded New England conservatism. Gone were the men who would take a chance on the future of their own city or who would make a sacrifice to save the prosperity of their state and region.
>
> This withdrawal and inertia of Boston's wealthy people and its business community conditioned the outlook on life of the Irish majority in the years from 1900 to 1940. Because the city did not enjoy the economic expansion that invigor-

ated other major cities, the Irish made very slow progress into the middle and upper classes. By the end of this period, only four of the thirty directors of the Boston Chamber of Commerce were of Irish descent. . . . Ethnic and class lines almost exactly coincided. The majority who had the political power felt themselves distinctly separated from the minority who had the economic power, and the separation was not only along economic lines, as it would be elsewhere, but also along nationality, religious and cultural lines. Moreover, the visible failure of the city to progress economically meant that the working class did not respect or have confidence in the business leadership even on the latter's own terms, that is, on economic terms. State Street could not reasonably assert that its stewardship of the economy had brought prosperity to the city.

Boston's population increased from 560,000 in 1900 to 780,000 in 1940. Since the economy did not expand, there was throughout this period, except briefly during World War I, a chronic labor surplus. The number of persons engaged in manufacturing remained virtually constant: 52,000 in 1900 and 57,000 in 1940. Approximately half those who had jobs were employed in comparatively low-paid and static occupations such as clerical and sales jobs, and domestic and service work. The occasional unemployment of manual laborers that had been familiar before World War I spread and became endemic in the city after the war. Throughout the 1920's when the rest of the nation was enjoying an economic boom, Boston regularly sustained an unemployment rate of 12 to 15 percent. The great depression of 1929 and afterward further narrowed the horizon and darkened the scene.

The Irish reacted to this economic squeeze by struggling to find a protected job in the civil service. The competition for openings as teachers, policemen, firemen, school janitors, and clerks became intense. Jobs in the large private monopolies such as the telephone and electric-light companies were equally desirable. Two of Boston's recent mayors exemplify this occupational pattern. Maurice Tobin, mayor from 1938 to 1945, began as a clerk and rose to divisional traffic manager for the telephone company. John Hynes, mayor from 1950 to 1960, began as a clerk in the city Health Department and spent twenty-nine years in the municipal bureaucracy. He was city clerk when he resigned to run for mayor in 1949.

Security and status became ruling obsessions for the Irish at their economic level as it had for the Back Bay Brahmins at theirs. Instead of sharing the more characteristic American attitude of confidence and optimism where material matters are concerned, the spirit that says there is "more where that came from" and plenty to spare for all, Boston developed the ethos of a civil service city. Too many Bostonians had the less attractive attitudes of the frustrated bureaucrat: "Pass the buck, don't stick your neck out and keep your nose clean." The lack of necessary economic and social elbow room made everyone hold rigid and tense as twentieth century Boston came gradually to resemble a giant subway car in the five o'clock rush: no space to move and every seat occupied even to the end of the line.

The Boston Yankees did not, of course, yield government and civil service without a fight, nor did the Irish Democrats maintain them since early in this century without occasional battles against the Good Government Association, the banks, and other Brahmin establishments. But over the years the genuine threat posed by these elements to the powers of the city became less and less substantial and increasingly ceremonial. It was good form for a Curley to remark that the term "codfish aristocracy" was an insult to the fish, or that in Boston the Caseys spoke only to the Curleys and that the Curleys would speak to whomever they damn well pleased. But those were gestures: no Brahmins were taking over. In fact they were taking off to other places and other concerns—to the suburbs, to nonpolitical reform associations, and to the vast network of charitable organizations, colleges, hospitals, moral uplift societies, and Puritanical watchdog associations for which Boston became justly famous. Concurrently they transferred as much power as possible to the legislature (from which, for a time, they tried to run the city), to the governor, and to the various special commissions. Sometimes they simply tried to diversify power, to spread it around in little indistinct piles so that the Irish would find it hard to gather. They abolished the ward basis of representation in city politics, making it necessary for all councilmen and school committee candidates to run at large, and they helped institute what they considered rigid civil service procedures. As a consequence power in city elections shifted to unexpected places—to city employees, for example, whose effect in endorsing and electing candidates has been substantial—and to the newspapers which became the locus for communication when the intimacy of personal acquaintance within the wards was removed. It was ironic that, in the 1965 School Committee election, a number of the reformers lamented the passing of the ward system; with it, the opponents of Mrs. Hicks might have elected at least one or even two members of the committee.

The history of the struggles of the Irish to establish themselves in Boston—despite the new styles and facades, and despite their long domination—still conditions life in Boston, its politics, its personal style, its restricted opportunities, and its occasional irreverence—analogous to an anticlericalism—in the face of hierarchical structures and authority. It is still exceedingly good practice for a politician, even one of the stature of Senator Teddy Kennedy, to march through South Boston in the Saint Patrick's-Evacuation Day Parade, and to get together on ceremonial occasions with lesser politicians for corned beef at one of the tribal eateries in South Boston. It is still standard practice—in case there is any doubt—to let the electorate know that a candidate is a Democrat and a Catholic with roots in the Emerald Isle (Italians can get elected from certain Boston wards, and they can achieve state office, but it is unlikely that they will come to dominate the city's politics). Boston is probably the only city in the world—certainly the only one in America—where a major newspaper can—in 1966—think of devoting an entire issue of its Sunday magazine to the Irish uprising of 1916, and where, in the year 1966, a person could declare in a letter to a newspaper:

> My education, both cultural and patriotic, was steeped in Yeats, Pearse, Plunkett and McDonough. As I grew to adulthood I heard over and over again fireside stories of the glorious Easter Rising and the 16 dead men.
>
> As an adult, and a naturalized American, I still hear those glorious tales today. The Irish take such a delight in weaving these historic tales of "terrible beauty."
>
> On Easter Sunday I marched through Boston with my fellow Irishmen to commemorate the anniversary of the Easter Rising. I listened in Faneuil Hall to the speeches and songs and

the reading of the proclamation and the rising rhythm of the "Soldier's Song."

Fellow Irishmen, the time has come to cease living in our "glorious" past; to stop our outflow of energy on our past heroes; let us remember them in silent prayer and use our energy for a new beginning of an old struggle for Irish independence.

Despite the fact that the city is 80 percent Catholic and probably 60 percent Irish, depending on how one counts, the Boston Irish still tend to act like a minority. They have called themselves the largest minority anywhere, and have been called, by others, the only oppressed majority in the world. Both descriptions are revealing because they help explain the controversies in which Boston has been recently embroiled. One Boston Negro leader describes the middle-class Irish as people without any sense of *noblesse oblige*, a politically potent majority who still act as if *they* were the victims of discrimination. Despite the position of the Church and of a growing number of liberal Catholics who are shedding their ethnic politics, the Negro militants, if they find any white allies at all, find them most often among upper-middle-class Yankees (who are generally secure financially and educationally), not among middle- or lower-middle-class Irish or Italians, and certainly not among the first generation Eastern Europeans who have appeared in Boston since World War II. Thus there has developed a new Protestant-Yankee-Negro alliance (joined by Catholics like Gartland and by suburban Jews) constantly asking the electorate and the politicians to yield in behalf of equality and social justice. Only an economically and socially secure population could respond to such appeals, and many of the Irish who still live in the city are not.

They live in Dorchester and South Boston (Southie), surrounding the Bunker Hill monument in Charlestown, and, if they have moved up, in West Roxbury or Hyde Park. Within the community, they, like all other groups, make severe distinctions. The lace curtain Irish at "The Point," the Eastern end of South Boston, look down on those who live on lower Broadway ("the other end") as people who "don't give a damn because they pay rent." The lower Broadway Irish are still stigmatized as an embarrassment to the community: "They're the ones who throw things at [civil rights] parades and who get drunk." And yet, despite these divisions, and despite the fact that large numbers of Irish families have gone to the suburbs (the South shore town of Scituate is sometimes called "the Irish Riviera"), the Irish population seems to remain more stable than most other "minorities." Although they came even later than the Irish, the Jews in Roxbury have—most of them—long moved on, either to suburbs like Newton and Brookline, or to newer Boston city areas like Mattapan, just across the line from suburban Milton. The Irish stay on, displaying a clannishness that seems to survive from generation to generation. Scott Greer, in a study of the modern metropolis, has pointed out that the social and religious activities of the good Catholic require a degree of spatial concentration:

> The early mass requires that church be not too far distant while the rule of thumb for location of elementary schools is that they be within a mile (walking distance) of the children's homes. Thus the Catholic is concerned, when looking for a residential neighborhood, with the accessibility of his organizational network. Furthermore, when he moves into a neighborhood where Catholics live in numbers sufficient to justify a church and school, he is likely to find relatives in the same area. Religious endogamy tends to produce, not only religious uniformity among kinfolks, but kin among fellow communicants. Thus the neighborhood with a heavy concentration of Catholics may exhibit a higher degree of neighboring and community organization than will ones of similar social rank and urbanism. *Concentration has results similar to segregation for the local area as a social system* [italics added].

The clannishness of the South Boston Irish explains in part the success of Louise Day Hicks and the area's strong commitment to the neighborhood concept. The Irish want to stick together, why don't the Negroes? And if the Irish can maintain good community order, can get ahead in the world, why can't Negroes? In a challenge like this, the phrase "getting ahead" assumes a special meaning, colored by Boston's civil service attitudes: the rows of plain South Boston houses—brown, green, gray, each occupied by two or three families—hardly reflect great success in "getting ahead" if one judges according to the standards of the average middle-class American. Nor do the better single and double family houses on the streets of Dorchester. But they do represent a restricted kind of security, a mortgage-paying stability, and, in the case of many parts of Dorchester, a large step up from South Boston. Above all, they reflect respectability. (Irishmen who have *really* made it seem to be viewed with a kind of double vision that betrays the ethnic inferiority complex that the Brahmins and the British have driven into the Irish. A man like John F. Kennedy—or even Gartland—who achieves social or economic standing is proof that the achievement is possible; but he also becomes, by virtue of the achievement, an outsider, almost a betrayer. Lace curtain Irish like Louise Day Hicks are still in sight and in the clan, but Harvard Irishmen are too far gone to belong.)

And yet neither clannishness nor Catholicism, nor any combination of the two, fully explains why the Irish are still where they are: that explanation lies at least in part in the historic lack of economic opportunities, in the civil service orientation it produced, and in the rural background of the Irish themselves. Daniel Moynihan, the political sociologist and former Assistant Secretary of Labor, has contrasted the Irish immigrants with the Jews—the one group of rural background, overwhelmed by the city, demonstrating all the forms of social pathology now appearing in the northern Negro ghettoes: high rates of crime, of alcoholism, of family breakdown; the other group historically urban, upwardly aspiring, highly ambitious, and strongly committed to education and to accumulating what Moynihan calls cultural capital. As a consequence the Jews—as much discriminated against as any other white minority—have tended to rise rapidly. The Irish have not.

The Irish, with their relatively more limited, hierarchical view, don't see why the Negro civil rights people are in such a hurry, are puzzled and frightened by Negro aggressiveness, overtly apprehensive as the ghetto slowly spreads south through Dorchester and west into Jamaica Plain, and impatient with all the sudden liberal concern for the Negro. Robert Coles, a psychiatrist who has thoroughly studied desegregation problems, quotes an Irish Bostonian:

> I know [the Negroes] had it bad here, but so did we all, my father and everyone else practically, except for the rich. And it's the rich, out there in the suburbs who keep on telling us what we should do. They preach at us to take them here and

35

let them live there, and act this way to them, and that, and so
on until you get sick of hearing it all. Suddenly they're so
kind, the suburban crowd. They stepped all over us, and kept
us out of everything, the Yankees and the college people over
there at Harvard did. Now they're so good. They're all excited
and worried about them. Talking about prejudice, that's what
we face, prejudice against *us*. I think we should start suing in
all the courts, and marching down those streets, like the Negroes.

There is a sense among the Irish, among the Italians, and among
other whites—as there probably is in every similar urban area in
America, that something is wrong with all the sudden concern for
the Negro, with the way he lives, and the schools he attends. No
one has ever had such concern for the poor whites, and no one,
they feel, has it now. Coles quotes an aspiring Boston politician:

> There's no glamor in white slums, only Negroe ones. The
> suburban housewives and the Ivy League students, they've
> gone poor-crazy, but only for the colored poor. . . . The minis-
> ters and the students come on Saturdays to tutor the Negro
> kids and take them to the park. They drive right by this neigh-
> borhood without blinking an eye. We have overcrowded
> schools. We have rotting buildings that should have been torn
> down years ago. We have lousy parks that aren't half the size
> they should be. A lot of people here have jobs that barely give
> them enough to get by; and the others, I'll tell you are on relief
> or unemployment checks or veterans' checks or something. We
> have our delinquents, our dropouts—the works. Who cares,
> though? Who has ever cared about this neighborhood? . . .
> It's a two-faced business, if you ask me, and it's becoming
> worse now that they talk about juggling our kids around so
> that they're "integrated." That's when you'll get the explosion
> here, when they try to move our kids across the city, or bring
> all those little darkies here. We've got enough, enough of our
> own troubles.

But this is a private feeling—and, when it comes to schools, not
very common. It is not public information, nor has it been the
cause for social action. Although the white schools may sometimes
be known to be overcrowded, and the parks inadequate, there has
been no articulate protest, perhaps because the very people (like

Mrs. Hicks) who express common fears about the Negro also re-assure those who have them that there isn't much wrong with the *status quo,* that the schools (for example) are in good shape. Many people share all the anxieties common to a lower-middle-class popu-lation which has never been socially or economically secure, and which has a sense that the ragged edge is not too far away: fear of economic competition, of declining real estate values, of disease, and crime, and lower standards of public service. Combine these fears with a smoldering resentment against the hypocrisy of Yankee suburbanites who insist that the poor white is responsible for in-tegrating the schools, and there is ample reason for intransigence, or even for something that the polls register as "bigotry."

The Boston Irishman, perhaps as much as any other lower-mid-dle-class American, is a person of compassion, of warmth, an in-dividual more interested in people than in generalizations and pro-grams. He has rarely been a racist; indeed, with his strong ethnic consciousness, he is usually proud of the good relations he has maintained with other faiths and races. But he does not see that he owes the Negro any special debt, and certainly cannot understand why the Negro should move into his schools, his job, or his neigh-borhood. Things haven't been that good to begin with. For him, good ethnic and social relations have always depended upon an almost medieval sense of order, with everything and everyone in his proper place. He has never regarded public education as an im-portant device for social or economic advancement—his sights have generally been limited to small goals anyway—and he there-fore can't understand what everybody finds so bad or so crucial about the schools. The schools provide discipline and order and jobs, they are less crowded than the parochial schools, and they are clean. Why is everybody complaining?

* * *

Blue Hill Avenue, which runs through the middle of the Rox-bury Negro ghetto, is sometimes known as agency row. Scattered among the second-hand clothing shops, the funeral parlors, and the establishments of the insurance peddlers, are welfare offices, youth centers, storefront churches, the outposts of the Northern Student Movement, CORE, Action for Boston Community Develop-ment, which handles most of the area poverty money, and Operation Exodus. On Sunday mornings sermons blare from evangelical church loudspeakers assuring the people that the Lord has great things for them in the next world, while, a few doors down, in the second-floor walk-up of the Blue Hill Christian Center, a militant Negro clergyman named Virgil A. Wood is telling his little congregation to "pray for power . . . If it is real worship," he says, "it ought to involve the body." Four girls stand awkwardly before the congregation singing "All over Boston, I'm going to let my little light shine," while, below, in the church's shabby little recreation center, the old men sit talking, or playing checkers, or just waiting.

Until a few years ago, when Boston's Negro population was not much above five percent, Blue Hill reflected the mixed population of the surrounding blocks: Negroes lived among Jews and Yankees, and even Irishmen, their children played together, and often attended the same schools. But Boston is now about 12 percent Negro, with the black population concentrated by housing discrimination and economic pressure into parts of the South End (not South Boston) and Roxbury. "Even if you have the money you can't find the housing," said Herbert Henderson, the president of an area parents group. "The banks will lend you $50,000 for a place in Roxbury or North Dorchester, but not a cent for the middle of town." As in other northern cities, considerable immigration from the South has accelerated the growth of the Negro population. "There's a myth in the South," Henderson said, "that Boston has good race relations and good schools. But I earn a good living and this is the best housing I can find. In Birmingham, this would be considered a slum."

The growth of the Negro population has converted Roxbury, once predominantly Jewish, into a predominantly Negro area, and the geographical limits of "Roxbury" have begun to spread. "The place now includes parts of what used to be called Dorchester and Jamaica Plain," said a long-time Negro resident, "because it's come to stand for the Boston ghetto. Roxbury is now like Harlem." Roxbury's detached two- and three-story frame houses bear little architectural similarity to Harlem's rows of brownstones, but in the conditions of life, in the peeling paint, the broken windows, the littered streets, it is very much a slum. The Boston Redevelopment Authority estimates that of the 27,000 dwelling units in Roxbury and North Dorchester, 34 percent are "deteriorating" and ten percent are "dilapidated." In the South End, a once-fashionable district that is now also part-ghetto, 45 percent of the homes are listed as deteriorating and another ten percent as dilapidated. Roxbury, with about one eighth of the city's total population, has more than half its 70,000 Negroes; the South End has most of the rest. In some districts of Roxbury, there are no whites at all.

With the growth of the city's Negro population and the national development of the civil rights movement has come a mounting awareness of racial injustice in Boston. Until a few years ago it was impossible to rouse the Roxbury community on any issue; race relations, given the standards of the days before Martin Luther King, were good in Boston. The city has never had a race riot and it has benefited for years from some of the most advanced antidiscrimination laws in the United States, most of them passed through the efforts of Jews and liberal Protestants. Boston was the city of Crispus Attucks, the Negro who is generally named as the first man killed in the American Revolution; and some of its Negroes can trace their ancestry back almost as far as the bluebloods, and can justly claim—if they wished—that they once looked down on the immigrant Irish. One Negro leader was incensed when someone told her that if she didn't like it in Boston, why didn't she go back to Alabama."My people," she said, "have been here a hell of a lot longer than that little son of a Paddy." Boston was the home of abolition, of William Lloyd Garrison, and *The Liberator*, and in Edward Brooke it has the highest-ranking Negro officeholder in America. (Until 1966, when he ran for the Senate, he was the state's attorney general.)

As a consequence of this euphoric history, and of the fact that the Negro population was so small, the Boston Negro remained politically and socially impotent. "I remember," said Mrs. Ruth Batson, the former education chairman of the NAACP, "that not too many years ago I had to sell my own committee on the idea that *de facto* segregation was bad." In Roxbury, as everywhere else, parents began slowly to discover that they were all in the same boat, that no child was learning very much, and that it wasn't simply because *all* the children were stupid. They discovered that their kids were being pushed and sometimes beaten in the schools (paddling is still allowed in Boston), that there were large numbers of temporary teachers, that many buildings were substandard, and that, as in other cities, performance in the ghetto schools, as measured in reading achievement and other scores, grew poorer the longer the children were in school. Some of the complaints were more imaginary than real; parents saw discrimination where there was none, and inferiority where teachers and principals were doing their utmost to surmount difficult physical or academic problems. Middle-class Negroes have become justifiably sensitive about references to Negro children as "culturally deprived," a phrase that has often become a euphemism for racial inferiority; at the same time it is a fact that many Negro children—because they are poor, and because their parents lack education, books, or even the middle-class language that is taken for granted in all schools—*are* culturally deprived. And yet the incumbent school administration, always highly defensive, did little to inspire confidence or improve communication, and thus seemed to confirm even the most unfounded complaints. As a consequence the growing list of grievances, coupled with the refusal of the School Committee to recognize the existence of *de facto* segregation, began to crystallize the community, helped fuel the school boycotts, and precipitated the formation of Exodus. The demands of the Negro leaders were relatively modest: they were directed, despite their occasionally intemperate tone, not toward large-scale reform, but merely toward winning public recognition from the School Committee that a problem existed. The NAACP—with its tradition of mild protest—was reluctant to participate in the first Boston school boycott (1963). A group of outsiders—Noel Day, director of St. Mark's Social Center in Roxbury, Alan Gartner, a teacher in Newton and a leader of Boston CORE, and several other militants pressured Kenneth Guscott, the president of the local NAACP chapter into support of the protest. These leaders, along with Ruth Batson and Paul Parks of the NAACP Education Committee, who were more militant than Guscott, were nevertheless aiming for a symbolic rather than a substantive victory. They wanted an admission that *de facto* segregation was a problem, and that efforts would be started to resolve it. The boycott was organized, Gartner said later, because "we didn't feel we could negotiate without troops." When the School Committee refused to yield, the Negro leadership achieved a second, though perhaps equally important, objective: they rallied the Negro community. "The best thing that ever happened to us," Melvin King said, "was Mrs. Hicks. She woke us up."

And yet, neither the boycotts, nor the School Committee election, nor even Exodus, has produced any major changes in the conditions of Negro life in Boston. All of them drew attention to the city's problems and all brought out people who had never been involved in community action before. King's campaign attracted several thousand new Negro voters and proved to be a triumph of ward organization: in some precincts more than 90 percent of the electorate turned out, voting for King and against Hicks by margins of fifty to one (252 to 5 in one Roxbury precinct, 562 to 13 in another); Exodus produced a corps of workers and planners who have become highly competent administrators and who have managed to raise $1,200 week after week to keep the buses running and the tutorials alive. Nevertheless, the Negro community remains frustrated, divided, and uncertain, despite its achievements. There is, understandably, more hostility in Roxbury now than at any time in history: white persons walking along Blue Hill Avenue, even in the daytime, have been spat upon, a form of aggression not novel in Watts or Harlem, but altogether new in Boston. (Mrs. Hicks has already declared that if there is a riot in Roxbury it will certainly not be her fault.) "Two years ago," said King, "we thought we were going somewhere. Now it turns out that nothing has happened and nothing has changed."

Yet the most serious problem is not frustration, but division and uncertainty. Roxbury is littered with fragmented organizations reminiscent of the religious splinter sects of the American South and West. For every grievance, a new committee is established, each with its own storefront office and its own little board of directors, many of them white intellectuals from the South End or Beacon Hill. (The South End is tipping uncertainly between middle-class rejuvenation and permanent decline into a slum. A few whites trying to bear witness to their commitment to integration—men like Prof. Harvey Cox of the Harvard Divinity School—have even moved to Roxbury.) Among the responses to the Hicks victory in the 1965 election, and to King's and Gartland's defeat, was a move to establish independent "public" schools in the ghetto, to "secede" from the city system. Three separate groups began discussions based on the feeling that since there was no hope for good education within the system then it would have to be achieved outside, but they never managed to get together and soon two of them gave up their efforts while the third—which came increasingly to be dominated by whites—started planning something that could only succeed with a highly motivated middle-class clientele. There are organizations devoted to tutoring, others to identifying children with special talents, and still others to various forms of community action, none of them with the ability or the resources to represent a significant portion of the community.

More important, however, has been the lack of any coherent policy for action, or even a consistent attitude. Since the 1965 election most responsible Negro leaders—men like King and Paul Parks, the current education chairman of the NAACP—have pinned their hopes on the state and federal governments, and have sensibly ceased trying to approach the School Committee altogether. Their expectation is that ultimately the withholding of funds under the Racial Imbalance Law or under existing or new federal legislation will hit the city where it really hurts. Simultaneously they have put pressure on Roxbury businesses, among them a supermarket and a building contractor, that were not employing Negroes or that discriminated against them in other ways. One store, they charged, was willing to cash checks for whites but not for Negroes. At the same time two Negro legislators from Boston have demanded that the city clean up the vacant lots in the ghetto, and that parks now littered with debris be provided with new facilities and made sufficiently attractive so that they will—and can—be used. And yet, at least until recently, they have not really made themselves felt, in spite of the growing population of the Negro community, because they are not sure—and this is true within the Negro protest movement at large—whether to demand equality or special opportunity, whether to ask for compensatory or parity education. Many Negroes in Roxbury are as opposed to busing for example, as are the Dorchester whites, a sentiment that the neighborhood advocates have often quoted against the civil rights people. Many Negroes are not certain whether to ask for a high quality academic program oriented to college admission or to follow the "realists" who insist that the major thrust be devoted to relevant vocational education and to developing job opportunities for skilled Negro labor. They are divided on the proper degree of militancy, with CORE generally at a radical extreme and the middle-class members of the NAACP at the other; they are not certain what makes all-

Negro schools *per se* inferior to all-white ones (assuming good faith on the part of the administration in allocating resources), are not certain what racial balance really means, and are emphatically confused on ways to achieve it in Boston. Recently the message of black power has been heard in the city, and been translated into a putative "Committee of 80,000 for Roxbury Self Help." In describing it, one of its spokesmen, the militant minister Virgil A. Wood, called it a way of making certain "that our concerns are communicated to the highest councils of government in our city and state. . . . Black power means the power to control our own destiny, just as others seek to control their own. We want the same kind of self-determination which drove the Boston Yankees up Bunker Hill to slaughter the British. The same thing the Irish wanted when they turned the Yankees out of city hall. The same thing DeValera wanted when he barricaded himself in the Dublin Post Office to rid his country of the English masters." Whether such a movement or any other organization can attract a substantial proportion of the Negro population—whether it can ever legitimately speak for all the Negro population—is a serious, and open, question. When Senator Edward Kennedy met with the Negro leaders of the city in the winter of 1965–66, he incensed them by telling them that they didn't know what they wanted, and that they had no chance of making any real progress until they had a consistent platform. So far, they don't have it.

There is no agreement anywhere on the solution for the problems of segregation and Negro deprivation, and Boston's Negro community, just beginning to feel its muscle, cannot be blamed for failing to unite behind a single approach. Nevertheless the fragmented Negro organizations, and the inconsistent messages they originate, make it clear that there is no universal Negro position— that no one alone speaks for all Negroes—and that, were it not for discrimination in housing, and perhaps in education, there would be no single Negro community at all.

* * *

Boston, it is often said, was laid out by the cows. Which, to paraphrase the honorable Mr. Curley, is an insult to the cattle. Through the years the city's best planning was a product of its conservatism while its worst was simply the consequence of the uncontrolled spread of neighborhoods that had developed from the little village centers along the valleys and railroad lines which gave access to the central city. Beacon Hill, the Back Bay with its magnificent Commonwealth Avenue, and the Boston Common which adjoins them, undoubtedly constitute some of the most pleasant and urbane areas to be found in any American city. For the people whose economic fortunes sufficiently exceed the magnitude of their family responsibilities—who have, in other words, more money than children—it is sometimes possible to live in a Beacon Hill Bulfinch House or in one of the low numbers on Commonwealth, and thus to have comfortable access to the city's richest resources: Locke-Ober's Restaurant, the Union Oyster House, Goodspeed's Book Shop, the shops and art galleries of Newbury Street, the Common itself. Edward Weeks, for many years the editor of the *Atlantic Monthly*, another Boston institution gone national, described how he walked to work every morning from his Beacon Hill residence "through the loveliest garden in North America." Within Boston, he said, is "the best orchestra in the world, the best hospital . . . the historic hospitality of Beacon Hill and the leadership of great universities." In the old North End, where the Paul Revere house still stands, there are magnificent narrow streets lined with Federal-style buildings now occupied by the Italians who came to the city a half century ago, and little groceries and bakeries and pharmacies marked Abruzzi, Roma, Fustaglia, with their open boxes of herbs and cans of olive oil and long salamis hanging in the windows—and, above, the women leaning out of the open second-story windows making conversation with the passersby.

But within Boston, too, is the decay of Roxbury and Charlestown with their dirty streets and broken glass and rusting cars, the sameness of the two-family tar-shingled houses in Roslindale, the endless monotony of Washington Street under the elevated tracks to the southwest. The Bunker Hill monument in Charlestown, presumably one of the city's greatest historical sites, is surrounded by shabby frame houses, a gray pile of a high school that looks like a tomb with windows, and the refuse of neglect. In the winter the kids, on pieces of cardboard, slide down the little rutted hill surrounding the monument, and all through the year the smoke and haze from the power plants and the nearby factories hang over the harbor to the east. Boston is almost surrounded by water, the

Charles River on the north, and the Bay to the east, yet almost nowhere is that water attractively accessible to human beings. Between the Back Bay and the Charles, with its boat basin and regattas, is the barrier of an arterial highway, while much of the Bay is blocked by warehouses and unused docks, by expressways and industrial installations. Where San Francisco has used its hills to superb residential advantage—each with a breathtaking view and with housing in which people *want* to live—Boston has covered them with undifferentiated two- and three-story structures (relieved here and there by little corner groceries) and with a street pattern showing little regard for the natural contours of the land. Boston does have distinct neighborhoods, but they depend far more on the ethnic background of the people who inhabit them—and who, more than elsewhere, have remained together—than on physical or architectural distinctions. A Dorchester high school student, asked if he wanted to move to another section of the city, remarked that there was no point: "Once you've seen one part you've seen it all."

Tying all this together is Boston's weird transportation system, a network anchored to the Massachusetts Turnpike, which terminates in the center of the city; to a system of arterial highways, often elevated, that separate parts of the city like Chinese walls, and that manage to disorient motorists with a jarring impact; and to the sickly Metropolitan Boston Transit Authority, a starving combination of ancient streetcars, buses, and subway trains rumbling along and under the streets according to a plan that can only be described by the frequent local injunction: "If you get lost, go back to Park Street and start over."

As a consequence of its residential poverty—itself partially a result of the middle-class exodus—the families who give strength to public institutions have moved into the suburbs. In this respect Boston shares the problems of every other American city, but it has them worse. Newton and Brookline, Wellesley and Lexington, Milton and Weston, have drained the core city of much of its talent and have established outstanding school systems thriving on the city's cultural blood. In the meantime the new industries that have come to the region since World War II, most of them in the electronics-brain bracket (attracted by the scientific establishment around M.I.T.) have settled along Route 128, the circumferential highway that rings Boston but never enters it.

Boston's suburbs, historically fearful of the city and jealous of their legislative power, have never given the city the resources it genuinely needs. Because the surrounding communities hold three-fourths of the metropolitan population and a vast absolute voting advantage on Beacon Hill, the city has never been able to get more in taxes and revenues than the potentates of the periphery permitted. The affluent city of Newton, for example, received, until recently, about three times as much state aid for schools per child as did the impoverished overtaxed city. Historically Boston was underrepresented on the Metropolitan Transit Authority which the suburbs ran to benefit themselves, and overtaxed in almost every department in which distinctions could legitimately be made. At the same time, the suburbanites, with the collaboration of a few Beacon Hill Brahmins and Cambridge academics, have lost few opportunities to remind the city of its inferior schools and its deprived Negroes. (No one has said much about the fact that even among the Negroes who could afford to do so few ever managed to break racial barriers in the lusher parts of Wellesley, Brookline, or Framingham.) The better people, who used to berate the Irish from right in town, have moved to the suburbs. But they have not changed their habits.

Boston has been paying the price of deprivation escalated by the cost of culture. More than 40 percent of all Boston real estate is tax exempt because it is held by churches, universities, and hospitals (among them the Massachusetts General, which may be the greatest medical center in the country). The real estate tax rate in 1966 was a staggering $115 per thousand dollars of valuation, probably the highest in the nation, and made higher still by the city's perennially high assessments. (One of the standard techniques of the old city politicians was to exchange tax abatements for political favors and campaign support.) These expenses made Boston even more unattractive to commerce (let alone residential development), and they threatened to drive even more of its assets away. There was a period some ten years ago when many people expected Boston to disappear as a vital physical entity and to remain as a place of significance only in folk memory, an economic Pompeii overwhelmed by an eruption of taxes.

The reversal started haltingly under the administration of John B. Hynes, the man who beat Curley for mayor in 1949 (and who beat

him twice thereafter) and then gathered momentum and effectiveness with the election of John F. Collins in 1959 (he took office in
1960). During Hynes' administration the city broke the legal ice
that led to the construction of the 52-story Prudential building and
to the redevelopment of the area surrounding it (a new hotel, an
auditorium, and other facilities). The key was a formula that ex-
empted the Prudential from normal city real estate taxes in exchange for 20 percent of the return on the building with an annual
guarantee of $3 million, and the key to *that* was to gain the accept-
ance of all parties, including the traditionally conservative Boston
business community. But the Prudential, which hardly alleviated
either the housing or the tax problem, was more symbolic than substantial. Thus, when Collins arrived in office in 1960 he started on
what at least appeared to be a new tack. Hiring Edward J. Logue,
who had successfully directed redevelopment in New Haven,
Collins began to back plans that emphasized rehabilitation as well
as razing and renewal, and that attempted to take advantage of the
city's assets, and especially of its reputation as a city of culture and
brains. He and Logue, through the Boston Redevelopment Authority,
began to promote Boston as—in their phrase—The City of Ideas,
and thus to try to attract the people and institutions who depend on
highly trained personnel, and especially on scientists and other
intellectuals. The program they planned was to combine the dramatic development of new areas with the rehabilitation of that housing and those sections they considered essentially sound—to bring
back the old neighborhoods. So far—and this despite the expend-
iture of huge sums in federal funds—the first part of the plan has
been more successful than the second. The Government Center is
being completed, a major new downtown office building (the State
Street Bank) has been finished, and there is a new upper-income
housing project near the Charles River in what used to be the old
West End. There are, furthermore, ambitious ten-year plans for
other major redevelopment projects, for improving and extending
the transportation system, and for rehabilitating older neighborhoods. In 1960, according to BRA calculations, 50,000 housing
units in the city—about one in five—were either dilapidated or
deteriorating. The city plans, in the period ending in 1975, to construct 37,000 new housing units and to succeed, through a combination of public and private initiative, in rehabilitating 32,000

others. In one part of Roxbury alone, the 186-acre Washington Park area, Logue and Collins hope to restore and improve more than 3,000 buildings now considered substandard but sound. The results have been mixed. In a few places in the South End white families have taken over old brownstones and are converting them into showcases of urban life, taking advantage of high Victorian ceilings, fireplaces, and circular staircases, developing little gardens in what used to be junk-filled back alleys, and generating new hope for what was at one time one of the city's more fashionable areas. In Roxbury some houses have grown new coats of paint and have been freed of the decay and trash that surrounded them. At the same time, however, neighboring buildings are crowded with two or three families and are pock-marked with broken glass, garbage, and cracking walls and stairways. In the South End, as in Roxbury, white hunters in new automobiles still cruise the streets looking for Negro prostitutes, while, on Columbus Avenue, on Washington Street, and on Blue Hill Avenue, the bars and honky-tonks offer neon-lit happiness to young men and women with no place to go. The new schools are still waiting to be built, the parks are still littered with junk, while the housing projects erected in Roxbury during the past decade—none of them listed as dilapidated in the statistics—already look like prisons.

Logue and Collins have had some success with what they call human urban renewal, but not nearly as much as with their dramatic building projects. Under Logue's leadership, the city established Action for Boston Community Development (ABCD), a general social agency supported by foundation and federal funds whose functions include—or were supposed to include—providing assistance to families being relocated in new housing, the direction and planning of neighborhood action programs, and the supervision of poverty projects, pre-kindergarten classes, youth employment, and a variety of other enterprises. But ABCD, like many other urban poverty agencies, has been embroiled in controversy and confusion and, for a time, appeared to be on the verge of dissolution. Logue himself became an ABCD critic because he felt the agency was not coordinating its efforts with those of the BRA. More important, the entire rehabilitation program—though it has made some progress—has not moved nearly as fast or as successfully as planned. Community resistance in some areas, failure to develop workable plans, and the general inertia of home owners, landlords, and neighborhood committees have blocked some proposals and delayed others. There is renovation, and there are plans and new organizations, but there are still very few major signs that Boston's older neighborhoods are significantly better than they were a decade ago. There has been little neighborhood integration, while racial tension, because of the school situation and the rising Negro population, is higher than it ever was. For several years Mayor Collins was successful in reducing the tax rate, but in 1966 it rose to its historic high of $115. There are no signs that large numbers of people have started to return to the central city and no signs—though here Logue certainly cannot be blamed—that the most important elements in renewal and redevelopment, the schools, have in any major way become more attractive. In an empty lot on Humboldt Avenue near the Washington Park renewal area stands a sign promising a new innovative elementary school. The sign was first erected in 1963; every year since then it has been updated. In the fall of 1966 the sign was still there, and the lot still vacant.

* * *

Boston's most significant form of renewal has come not from physical development nor from any tangible shift in population figures, tax rates, or racial integration, but from what appear to be new attitudes and a new set of political and social relationships. The city's various commissions and committees, its action organizations and planning groups, now include Harvard academics as well as Irish politicians, Brahmins as well as priests. In most other northern cities that kind of representation is hardly new: almost every city planning group or study committee in America includes a Jew, a labor leader, a Catholic, a woman, and perhaps a Pole, an Italian, or a Negro. But for Boston even this sort of ticket balancing is something of a novelty. Since the city's ethnic politics have generally involved two-sided struggles—or even one-sided struggles (usually between Yankees and Irishmen)—there have rarely been opportunities for establishing pluralistic ethnic arrangements involving representatives of several groups. There is a story of the leader of a Boston longshoremen's union who was shaving at his flat early one afternoon; his mother asked him why he was home so early.

"I'm going to give a speech at Boston College with Ralph Lowell, the banker, and some big-shot professor from M.I.T.," he replied.

"Oh, my God, John," said his mother. "You've been drinking again."

The new style, by no means universal, has brought together old Yankees with Dorchester Irishmen, North Boston Italians, League of Women Voters ladies, Chamber of Commerce people from the suburbs, priests, politicians, and planners. Msgr. Francis J. Lally, editor of the archdiocesan paper *The Pilot*, and a close associate of the Cardinal, is chairman of the BRA, while the Cardinal himself signs pronouncements and reports on racial balance; Charles Coolidge, a Brahmin attorney, was responsible for developing the tax formula that brought the Prudential Center to the city, and he has served on other redevelopment projects since; Gerald W. Blakeley, head of the lofty old-line real estate firm of Cabot, Cabot and Forbes, reestablished channels of communication between the city and the business community that had been closed since the days of the first Irish mayors; Harvard professors now enter City Hall while engineers and architects from M.I.T. have been widely involved in almost every phase of Boston's development. The Collinses and the Kennedys have replaced the Curleys as the city's archetypal politicians, while the Lowells are better known as backers of Boston's outstanding educational radio and television station than for icy isolation with the Cabots. The newness rests in a kind of ethnic and social ecumenicism, in the returning interest, if not yet the returning presence, of people who gave the city up, and in what might be described as a *sense* of renewal. No one can determine whether the concern is simply shallow economic opportunism masquerading as civic responsibility, and whether the concern for people and the conditions of life will be as substantial as the concern for commerce. Something has begun to stir in Boston: the old economic and political forms cannot survive forever. But no one can yet assess the staying power of the habits they created or the forms that will replace them when the old order fully disappears.

AT THE Boston School Department, encrusted in a ten-story spittoon-age building at 15 Beacon Street and in some 200 elementary and secondary schools, the old order is still intact. It is a world unto itself. The changes in political and ethnic style that are altering the rest of the city's public life have left the School Department virtually untouched. At 15 Beacon, where they are crammed into drab green cubicles with their secretaries and mimeograph machines, the McDonoughs still speak mainly to the O'Learys, the Caseys, and the Hogans, directing the work of 68 Sullivans, 61 Murphys, 21 Lynches, 18 Kelleys, 14 Kellys, 25 Walshes, 30 O'Briens, 40 McCarthys, 22 Dohertys, 21 McLaughlins, and some 3,700 other teachers and administrators, most of whom are Irish. Their Irishness—political, parochial, and often magnificently personable— has given the schools of the city problems and qualities that make them distinctive and sometimes notorious in American education. While Boston—and the nation—are bemused, fascinated, and sometimes horrified by the politics of the School Committee, the professional administrators (and the teachers they direct) carry on much as they have for thirty years. School committees come and go, the urban situation changes, there are new problems, a new technology, and a new class of kids; but the administration and staff go on, it seems, forever. While they are acutely aware of the middle-class exodus, of the lack of children with what they consider proper motivation, they still operate on the premises of another age, and on the fading laurels of a once-glorious reputation derived from an educational history that, for better or worse, is unmatched in America.

Operating alongside a parochial system that has profoundly influenced them and that has helped educate perhaps a third of the city's population, the public schools suffer from a tax base that has failed to keep pace with rising educational costs, from traditional legislative parsimony in providing state aid, and—until recently, when it was revised—from a state formula that provided more financial assistance to the affluent suburbs than it did to the inner city. Until 1966, when the Massachusetts legislature voted a sales tax and adopted a more equitable, and generous, plan for assisting Massachusetts cities and towns in financing public education—promising Boston more than $16 million a year in current operating funds (about 30 percent of the school budget) and another $16 million in construction aid, all in jeopardy because of the city's failure to comply with the imbalance law—Boston derived only ten percent of its school support from the state. The rest came from the local property tax. (In some states, state funds support more than 60 percent of local school budgets.) The Boston schools, moreover, are subject to an increasing number of deprived children, and the school system has been saddled with constitutional divisions of authority that give City Hall, rather than the School Committee, a major and sometimes decisive voice in budgetary matters and new school construction. The mayor may veto any school budget that exceeds the previous year's, and he has tended to dominate the three-man School Buildings Commission, which had final authority over new school construction. (The mayor and the School Committee each appointed one member of the Commission; these two elected the third member, but since the School Committee is prone to internecine warfare, and since the mayor had more influence and patronage, he effectively controlled the Commission. In the fall of 1966 the Commission was replaced by an independent Public Facilities Commission that was established to eliminate red tape, but which has not yet managed to expedite the city's glacial school construction program.)

Boston's school budget is roughly comparable to those of similar cities; the system spends about $500 annually to educate each child, approximately two thirds as much as New York, but no less than Chicago, Milwaukee, Seattle, or Pittsburgh. At the same time, however, the neighboring suburbs—Newton, Lexington, Wellesley —each of them with fewer social problems inside, or outside, the schools, spend well over $600, while really lush greenbelts like Scarsdale and Great Neck, both near New York, exceed $1,000 each. The Boston system, like those of many other northern cities, has been drained for years of its talented and motivated children, and it has been torn between two sets of educational enterprises that leave it more and more in a have-not condition. The parents of the average child in Newton have two to three years more education than the parents of the Boston child; in Newton the educated and the ambitious send their kids to the public schools; in Boston—if they can afford it—they send them to private (and sometimes parochial) schools. The glorious prep-school records of Exeter and Groton, of Andover and St. Paul's, and the achievements of Newton and Brookline, reflect the resources and motivation that the city exports. As in many other urban areas, public education in the core city has increasingly become dependent on what is essentially a system of pauper schools.

Because of the Boston Latin School, founded in 1635 and still the pride of the system, Boston can legitimately claim to have the oldest public school establishment in the nation. For generations rigid Yankee schoolmasters operated strict classes according to the Latin tradition, teaching grammar and algebra, Greek and composition, history and character. They established exacting standards of behavior, dress, and punctuality, and while—in the words of one teacher of long memory— "there were a good many Ichabod Cranes among them," they developed styles and standards that gave Boston a reputation as one of the outstanding school systems in America, a reputation that some of its defenders stoutly insist is still deserved. In the twenties, when only one child in ten in America actually finished high school, Boston's ratio was about one in three; those who did finish were admitted in vast numbers to the best colleges and universities in America. In 1932 the Latin School sent more boys to Harvard than any other institution, public or private, in the United States. Concurrently the city's trade schools were models for industrial education elsewhere in the country. Then, as the old masters began to retire, and as social conditions in the United States began to change, time stopped in the Boston schools.

The Irish who began to take over the system forty years ago, first as teachers, and later as administrators, rarely brought liberalism or reform. More often they came with attitudes formed in a conservative church and in a parochial establishment more rigid than the classic masters of the Yankee tradition. Beginning in the twenties there developed a network of informal but powerful interconnections between the parochial and the public systems. Teachers trained in the parochial schools taught in the city schools, regular staff members of one took moonlight jobs in the other, and administrators from the Boston system served as lay faculty at Boston College, Regis, and Emmanuel, where the majority of the area's Catholics received their formal teacher training. In 1929 William Cardinal O'Connell, then archbishop of Boston, urged strictest adherence to a papal encyclical condemning progressivism and declaring that every method of education "founded on the denial or forgetfulness of original sin and of grace, and relying on the sole powers of human nature, is unsound." In the same year a prominent committee of laymen who studied the public schools warned against "unwarranted expansion of new curricula" and against "eliminating established practices or policies." These two voices of conservatism, one ethnic and religious, the other political and economic, brought the city's embryonic experiments with new ideas to an abrupt halt. Concurrently, as the Irish took over the city and the schools, municipal reformers, fearing political shenanigans, enveloped the whole system with rigid civil service routines and at-large school committee elections, making minority representation and professional deviation almost impossible. In 1935, the Superintendent of Schools, Pat Campbell, was able to declare that "we do not need to teach the current economic theories, nor the ever-changing experiments in government nor the science of tomorrow. Let us remember that man must always learn from the experience of the past." In Boston, therefore, the spirit of John Dewey made few substantial inroads. At the same time, the style of the church and the parochial schools—which are themselves now beginning to change—was never far away.

Boston, the critics charge, is inbred. And with minor exceptions the charge is true. The majority of the city's teachers and administrators share similar lower-middle-class backgrounds, attended the same public or parochial schools, and graduated from the same colleges: Boston Normal, now Boston State, or one of the city's Catholic institutions, Boston College, Regis, and Emmanuel. Because of the celibacy patterns of the Irish—derived from the chronic Irish land shortage and the resulting need to postpone marriage, sometimes permanently, until the family place became available—and because Boston was among the last cities in America to permit married women to teach, the city still has a large proportion of maiden schoolmarms who, like their male colleagues, believe first in discipline and character, and who recognize curiosity and originality through the sometimes clouded lens of their limited backgrounds, their rigidity, their celibacy, and their civil service outlooks. Sometimes they have been compared, and not altogether favorably, with the nuns who staff the parochial schools, and have privately been described as classroom tyrants adept at the psychological emasculation of those young boys who become too assertive. But they can also be highly concerned and competent teachers, and extremely personable individuals with considerable warmth and charm. Almost inevitably they appear to be strong-minded people who have little difficulty controlling a class. They are, in short, all a little like Mrs. Hicks.

Compared to the senior administrators, the ethnic and cultural backgrounds of the teaching staff are positively pluralistic. Among the teachers are a few Italians and Jews, a handful of Negroes—about one teacher in two hundred is a Negro—even one or two Jewish principals. (Boston's first Negro principal was named in the fall of 1966.) But among the veterans at 15 Beacon, there is little such variety. All but one member of the Board of Superintendents, the senior staff of the system, are graduates of Boston College, all have risen through the ranks and have been in the system for more than three decades, all are well over 50 years old, all are Catholics, and all, excepting only Superintendent William H. Ohrenberger with his German background, are Irishmen. It is not possible for anyone to become a principal or an assistant superintendent in Boston without having first taught there, and it was only recently that the city began to recruit actively for new teachers outside the traditional list of feeder colleges and outside the Boston area. One leading critic, himself a Catholic, has privately called the administration "a bunch of real Romans, responsive to authority, and always prepared to take orders." To succeed in

Boston, he said, "you have to be a Catholic. It would be unthinkable to hire a non-Catholic as superintendent. This is a closed system. They never go outside and they never let outsiders in." Operating under the Irish Catholic-dominated School Committee, the senior administrators have often been represented as a closed club of unimaginative civil servants lacking interest in outside ideas, lacking contact with the city's great universities, and lacking initiative to innovate in anything but the most perfunctory manner. Ohrenberger himself, it is sometimes said, is not fully accepted by some of his staff because he is not Irish, although, with his background as a Boston College football player and four decades in the system, he qualifies in every respect but name. "The career people are what make the system tick," said one of the associate superintendents. Then he added, significantly, "the worst thing here is to imagine that you're going to be able to think. Everything is growing too fast. We don't have time to think."

There is a coziness in the green rabbit-warren offices at 15 Beacon, a personable affinity between people who have worked together for years, and who expect to maintain those relationships for the rest of their lives. Here are the patterns of the small village, of the city ward, of the parish, with their strong kinship ties and their personal concerns: whose mother has just gone to the hospital, whose daughter will be married next month, whose son is entering the army. This is a world not only of McDonoughs and Hurleys, but of Marys and Johns, of cousins and nephews and sons. "There used to be more of a spirit of warmth," said an administrator recently, lamenting the harassment produced by new courses and new Federal programs. "It's getting like a big corporation." But in the offices and elevators, in the halls and the street outside the building, the little clusters of people continue to exchange their personal news and their occasional remarks of irreverence made secure by the hierarchical structure and the stability it provides: friendly, close, comfortable. And this feeling often extends not only to fellow administrators, to principals, and to teachers, but, at its best, to the children and to the system as a whole. Given the political limitations imposed by the School Committee, the administration is more competent and concerned than the voters have any right to expect. Ohrenberger does not fight the committee, but he has usually pushed as far as his capricious bosses have allowed: he recommended busing to relieve overcrowding, he initiated the collaborative programs with Harvard and the Office of Program Development, and he was responsible for beginning almost all of the compensatory and experimental programs—minor as many of them are —which the city now conducts. When Ohrenberger speaks about the morale of the staff he is, on the whole, probably correct. He and his associates have had to manage an aging system while school committees played politics above them; they have had to run a decaying plant while, at the same time pretending—for the sake of public relations, and for the sake of their own pride—that everything was all right. Here is the morale of the beleaguered fortress standing off the attackers, the morale of people with long personal and professional associations, the morale of the going concern. There is genuine feeling in the voice of Marguerite Sullivan who was, until her retirement in 1966, the deputy superintendent. "Sometimes it's hurt to be a political football," she said, reflecting on almost a half century in the system. "But we have always been concerned with the children, concerned with building values. No matter what happened in the politics of the School Committee, the system has always operated according to the highest ethical standards." She, like Ohrenberger, like other members of the staff, speak of Boston's impersonal, objective standards of appointing and promoting teachers, its examinations and point scales, its rigid rules and practices governing advancement within the system. The School Committee cannot originate recommendations for promotion; only the Superintendent has that power, they say. There is no inbreeding; the School Department was only the victim of old regulations requiring its teachers (at one time) to live in Boston, and of the depression-era influx of Boston College graduates; and it is now recruiting all over the nation. At every criticism of inbreeding the administrators quote figures for how many people took the last test, how many passed, and how many took jobs in Boston. They do not point out that the impersonal "objective" selection and promotion procedures—if properly used—tend to attract more of the same kind of people and that the more methodical the routines are, the less room is left for deviation and originality. The city's teacher examinations, required of all candidates, no matter what their experience, and administered only in Boston, favor people with text-book minds who can regurgitate the facts of their subject. In American history, for example, applicants are asked:

On an outline map of the United States:
a) trace the route of the Erie Canal, naming and locating its terminal cities.
b) trace the route of the Santa Fe trail, naming and locating its terminal cities . . .

Match each of the individuals listed in the first column with the historic incident or book associated with him and listed in the second column:

D. G. Farragut   The Alamo
Davy Crockett   Black Friday
Jim Fiske   Capture of New Orleans
    (etc.)   (etc.)

Why is the Senate a much more influential body than the House of Representatives?

What aspect of the makeup of the Senate is open to serious criticism?

Each of these questions can be answered by someone who has studied a high school textbook; none requires genuine historical skills, ability to deal with historical materials, or any real sense of the techniques and limitations of the field. Thus the very procedures designed to prevent political abuses also tend to stamp new personnel with the old image and to orient them toward accepted ways: adherence to textbooks, old techniques, and the conventional wisdom. It is harder to select teachers than postmen or sewer inspectors; yet Boston sometimes claims that it can be accomplished in the same manner.

In fact, Boston rarely does it that way. The rigid procedures are tempered with a personal style, with the private knowledge that an old self-perpetuating staff accumulates, and with the experiences of people who know that the world cannot be organized solely according to points, forms, and procedures. As a consequence the Boston School Department is really composed of two administrative networks, one formal, official, and apparently impersonal, the system that some civil service reformer dreamed about a half century ago; the other familiar, often friendly, and, in its own way, far more efficient. Without *it*, the system probably could not function at all. There is an incredibly rapid unofficial grapevine, reporting to administrators and certain members of the School Committee information which normal channels could accommodate only with the greatest difficulty, if at all. A Harvard professor, speaking at a summer seminar for teachers at a nearby university, makes some uncomplimentary remarks about the School Committee's attitude about segregation. Before the seminar has ended—while the professor is still talking—the remark has been reported to Mrs. Hicks, who calls the professor as he leaves the building. (If that's the way he feels, she says, Boston will no longer participate in the seminar.) A teacher, with apparently good reports from her superiors, is not rehired because she does not believe in filing lesson plans (making her, by definition, an inadequate teacher). There is no dissent among staff members; no one can remember the favorable reports. A custodian who has been ill for almost six months is granted another extension of his sick-leave with pay because everyone concerned somehow knows that this particular man is especially in need of help. A principal, who has just refused to admit a child under the open enrollment transfer regulations because there is no more space, receives a call originated by a legislator or a School Committee member and discovers that he does have a few seats after all and will be glad to accommodate the child.

Within this informal system there are special precincts—individuals to whom certain subordinates are especially loyal or who act as a kind of shadow staff for particular members of the School Committee. One administrator was described as "the head of the old maids' club. She has a group of people who go directly to her, and she enjoys tremendous loyalty from them. She takes care of her people."

No one has ever accused the administrators or the School Committee of malfeasance, of taking bribes or payoffs, or even of flagrant favoritism. "Nobody on this School Committee," said a long-time critic, "is on the take." There are no charges of nepotism, no accusations even that the administration favors the relatives of School Committee members. (The brothers of two incumbent members, Eisenstadt and McDonough, and Charles F. [Fred] Reilly, the brother of the former chairman, Madeleine Reilly, and Miss Reilly herself, all teach in the system. Miss Reilly was hired after her defeat for re-election in 1961.) And yet, the informal network within the system makes it apparent that the administration has not only captured the civil service system, but has learned how to use it. The machinery does not always work well, though it is probably as effective in abuse as in use. At any rate, it works better than the defensive administrators—often more Puritanically sanctimonious than the most severe Yankee—would like people to know. As they represent it—impersonal, mechanical, formal—it could hardly work at all.

* * *

The weak-watted lights, the electric clock on the wall, the green paint and Spartan brown chairs, make the meeting room of the School Committee into something resembling a small-town bus depot on the night of a blizzard. On the platform at the front of the room, Committeeman Joseph Lee, the old Yankee with the Ben Franklin glasses, has just completed a three-minute disquisition on the relation between productivity and the money supply, having earlier pointed out how "the mayor pays people to be idle." He now reaches into a crumpled paper bag, takes out the hookah he always carries to these meetings, and lights it. To his right, in a little circle behind their desks, sit the chairman, Tommy Eisenstadt, young, rather small, studying the papers before him with what someone has described as a "fox-terrier look"; Bill Ohrenberger, the superintendent, announcing, in his bulldog voice, a statement beginning, "Mr. Chairman and members . . . "; Bill O'Connor, at 66 becoming more prosaic and limited, leaning back to hear the message that his secretary is about to deliver to him; and John McDonough, young, tall, and still somewhat of an uncommitted, unknown quantity in his first months in office. Directly across from McDonough, on Joe Lee's left, sits Mrs. Hicks.

This is the Boston School Committee at its fortnightly meeting, looking vaguely like a discussion panel recruited by a small city television station that can't afford high-priced talent. To the committee's left, in two rows resembling a jury box, sit the genial bureaucrats, waving greetings to friends in the audience, and occasionally—when asked by Ohrenberger or a member of the committee—responding with a piece of information, a prediction, or a comment. In the small audience before the panel—and beyond the press table—are the representatives of the Home and School Association, the Citizens for the Boston Schools, the teachers' union, and the custodians' association, a few people hoping for a promotion, and whatever outsiders have been called to do business with the committee. Occasionally this dark chamber—sometimes described as rescue mission Gothic—has been jammed with spectators and protestors, but normally its one hundred seats are two-thirds empty.

It is impossible adequately to describe these meetings: they are, among other things, filled with lengthy ex cathedra declarations on almost every topic imaginable; they are frequently irrelevant, and they are constantly, pathetically, amusing. Since Arthur Gartland's defeat new alliances have started to develop. On the one side are Mrs. Hicks and O'Connor, staunch defenders of the racial *status quo*, adamantly rejecting all suggestions that the system redraw school district lines or bus children for the purpose of alleviating imbalance. Although the district lines were drawn in 1909, Mrs. Hicks and O'Connor are certain that any tampering will jeopardize the security of the precious neighborhood principle; they have promised neighborhood groups in Dorchester and elsewhere that they will never vote to change the patterns, and they honor the promise by their votes in the School Committee—even though state funds are already being held up, and may be withdrawn indefinitely. Adopting a moderate position are Eisenstadt, the current committee chairman, and McDonough. (Eisenstadt was elected chairman partly because he promised to make meetings brief and partly because—following the tradition of rotation—he has never been chairman before.) Eisenstadt modified his position on racial imbalance after the 1965 election, and some people have therefore become even more emphatic in calling him an opportunist. "It doesn't matter what I think," he said in explanation, "it's only a matter of complying with state law." Under his leadership, the committee, by a 3–2 vote, altered the rigid anti-busing stand to which he himself first led it in 1965. Now the committee is committed, at least in theory, against busing only if pupils are transported for the "sole purpose" of relieving racial imbalance. Eisenstadt is more aware than the other committee members—or at least more willing to admit—that the system has severe problems; in private conversation he can be vocal about the inbreeding of the administration. "I thought when I was elected," he said once, "that I could help reform the system. Now I know how hard it is. They can't tolerate anything that's really different." For Eisenstadt, who knows that the system is political ("you read in the papers that you have a lot of power and you begin to believe it"), the road to long-term success can only lie in moderation. He cannot play the great mother, and he is neither flashy nor callous enough to be a good demagogue, so that his future almost necessarily depends on a reputation for reason. "By resolving to conduct the affairs of public education in Boston with a new dignity, a new sense of equity, and impartiality, and by making a commitment to moderation in temper," he declared grandly when he took over as chairman, "we shall be setting the stage for solid progress, paving the way for monumental educational achievements that will serve to restore (a verb Mrs. Hicks would never use) the Boston public schools to their pre-eminence among the community of school systems throughout the nation." Eisenstadt has some pride in the small improvements he believes he helped start—expansion of the hot-lunch program, and of formal guidance and psychiatric services, and he hopes that the racial issue will fade from public attention; it can help Louise Hicks, but it can only drag him, and the system, through more trouble. His future, if he has one on the committee, lies in a record of improving education.

Between the two sides—Mrs. Hicks and O'Connor, Eisenstadt and (probably) McDonough—sits the hookah-smoking maverick Joe Lee, a Harvard Yankee who is the son of the man who became known as the patron saint of Boston's park system. Lee is one of the two members (the other is O'Connor) known to have no political ambitions other than to serve on this committee. In return Lee uses his seat as a platform for the exposition of views on everything from urban planning to the money supply. To him airplanes are still "flying machines," the State Commissioner of Education is guilty of "misfeasance" and should be fired, and recipients of welfare subsisting "on kindly payments from the public treasury" should be *ordered* to receive training in marketable skills. Lee, quite logically, feels that the only place to bus Negro children is to the white suburbs, that busing within the city will solve few problems, that the construction of major highways through residential areas is insane, and that one of the things the city needs most is opportunities for children to play and exercise. "Joe," someone said, "is always trying to restore the Boston he knew as a boy. It's an admirable wish." For more than a year the committee argued about the site for a new 5,000-student campus high school first proposed in 1962 and now desperately needed. (Hicks and O'Connor wanted it constructed outside the slums; Eisenstadt and McDonough favored a site more likely to comply with state racial balance requirements.) In February 1966, to satisfy Lee, who was, in return, willing to support them on the choice of location, Eisenstadt and McDonough voted for an order specifying that the new high school be built with a gymnasium accommodating all students *at once*. The following, by a 3–2 vote, thus became the official policy of the Boston School Committee:

> ORDERED, that the (Madison Park area) be designated as the school district within which approximately 60 acres of land should be taken on which to construct a campus-type high school to accommodate 3,000 pupils within doors, and to accommodate the same number of pupils at play at one time upon its grounds outdoors, said outdoor facilities to be designed specifically for the recreation and exercise at one time of 3,000 students, and said buildings likewise to be designed to include roofed gynmasia adequate for the participation in games by the same 3,000 students at one time, and the design to leave room for the construction later of additional buildings to accommodate 2,000 additional pupils, to a total of 5,000 all together, but to then provide or leave intact outdoor and indoor sports facilities which shall be at least sufficient all together in combined use to accommodate 5,000 pupils in their sport at once . . .

Most of Boston's educational problems were not created by this committee: they were inherited from years of neglect and apathy, from a historic conservatism, and from the very individuals who now proclaim themselves reformers. Suburbia thrives on people who can afford to escape from the city rather than reforming its education system, while the city itself is full of the clients of private and parochial schools. Until recently, few of the region's great universities took much interest in the public systems just beyond their walls, while their graduates, if they became teachers at all, trooped off to the greenbelts. The *Boston Herald*, which recently published a scathing series condemning the schools as "BAD," not many years ago editorialized against increased school budget appropriations and serious programs of academic innovation. ("It is to be hoped," said the *Herald* after World War II, "that the Boston School Committee will refrain from joining [the] rush to the modern. . . . A school building is not bad because it is old.") Mayor Collins himself—despite his constant professions of interest in good education—has cut requests for school budget increases. When it comes to education he sometimes seems as committed to inaction and nonprogress as the five people who are otherwise responsible for the system's $50,000,000 budget.

But if the School Committee has inherited problems, it also seems to have inherited an inability to confront or solve them. The masters of Beacon Street consistently involve themselves in discussions and controversies, in distractions and side issues that obfuscate and disregard the agonies of the system. With the collusion of the administrators, they engage in elaborate games, in formalized rituals about "our dedicated teachers" and "our wonderful system," and in elaborate strategies of defense against critics. (If Louise Hicks plays to any constituency, it is to the system's 7,000 employees.) When the *Boston Herald* series first appeared, Ohrenberger and the committee spent the better part of an hour denouncing it at a formal meeting, demanding retractions, and insisting on an opportunity to refute the charges:

> An end of patience has been reached [Ohrenberger declared in a three-page statement]. Our school system cannot continually turn the other cheek while our critics carp about our shortcomings, glorify our weaknesses and conveniently disregard our strengths. To continually allow public confidence in our schools to be eroded by malicious criticism without refutation or explanation would be unfair to the thousands of teachers and school personnel who give unceasingly of their time and effort to insure a sound education in this city. . . . I have constantly reiterated my commitment and that of my staff of dedicated teachers to the pursuit of excellence in the classrooms of this city.

"I'm perfectly satisfied with the schools," observed O'Connor,

who sometimes sounds like a Gaelic Polonius. "I think the superintendent should know that we have the greatest faith in the Boston schools."

"I think this is a terrible indictment of a wonderful system,"
Mrs. Hicks said in her singsong voice. "We should call for a boycott if the series continues."

"The *Herald* is a foreign paper," Lee added. "It is read only in
the suburbs; it would better be called the *Hingham Hiccough.*"

"We should give the superintendent a vote of confidence,"
O'Connor rejoined. "We should give him the physical and financial
support he requires to answer this."

The endless irrelevancies drift into every conceivable public and
private issue. Into lengthy discussions of urban renewal:

> *Lee:* We now have a foray against our own citizens right
> here in Boston. We must defend the people of Roxbury from
> this proposed invasion of their homes. If this highway is built
> we will need a refugee camp for all the displaced people.

And personal trivia:

> *O'Connor:* Having known him since he was a young boy
> going to English High School and having followed his prog-
> ress through the school system, I really find that he is a great
> asset, and I know, Mr. Superintendent, he will serve you well.
> He is loyal, devoted to his work . . .

Sometimes, even when the discussions are relevant, they blossom
into fruitless inconclusion, into a never-never land of futile rhetoric:

> *Lee:* We must help open up those trades. Young Americans
> are seeking a livelihood. This is a terrible hardship on our Ne-
> gro people.
> *O'Connor:* We still have enough problems without trying
> to fight the unions.
> *Lee:* Now, the longshoremen's union; they can't talk civil
> rights and then close the door to people trying to make a liveli-
> hood. If we can't take them on, how can a youngster fight for
> his rights? Let's extend a hand of cooperation.
> *O'Connor:* Oh, I don't mind that. . . . Once we provide the
> product, then they will open the gates.
> *Lee:* I haven't seen one colored man on the construction
> gangs down there at the new city hall . . .

Every member of this committee is an independent operator, playing to his constituency—internal and external, to the press, perhaps to his own vanity. There is no sense of urgency, no motive force. Meetings go on and on, transacting routine business, debating racial imbalance and redistricting from already-committed positions, uttering pieties about "our dedicated teachers" and "our wonderful schools," hurling invective at the mayor, at the State Board of Education, at urban renewal, at the state highway program, patronizing Negroes and teachers and children and each other. For two years the city has not built a single new school, even though $29 million in construction funds has been approved by the mayor and city council. There has been constant conflict between this committee, the mayor, and the School Buildings Commission, the three-member board which has authority over new construction, and which is controlled by the mayor. As a consequence of this magnificent piece of constitutional gerrymandering, responsibility for inaction perambulates, via endless memos, letters, and public declarations, between Beacon Street and School Street where, pending completion of the new city hall, the mayor hangs his hat. More than a third of the city's schools are over fifty years old; several are now into their second century, while 18 of the 20 schools that are more than 90 percent Negro were built before World War I. Dilapidated structures, some of them overcrowded and ill-used, litter the older neighborhoods. The city needs a new high school, a new trade school, more guidance counselors, more modern vocational programs, and, more than anything else, a full-dress discussion of the curriculum, the attitudes of teachers and administrators, of the way things are taught, the courses taught, and the people who teach them. It must seriously confront the question of what constitutes relevant urban education, and how it can be achieved—despite the division of power regarding construction, despite the suburbs, and despite antiquated buildings. But this School Committee, like most of its predecessors into the recesses of time, has never become sufficiently concerned to rouse the city's population, to dramatize the plight of rotting buildings and stagnant minds; rather it operates to deaden interest, to reassure the anxious, and to stifle the critics. In Pittsburgh the administration publishes pictures of obsolete buildings in an effort to rally public support for new construction, fliers are issued describing the inadequacies of the system, and the annual school report contains a candid description of *de facto* segregation, along with the school board's hopes for mitigating it. But not in Boston. Instead of calling administrators to task for their failures, the School Committee colludes with them to obscure and deny: if it genuinely wants new buildings—as its members claim—why don't they spend their living hours dramatizing the news—to the mayor, to the papers, to anyone who will listen—rather than praising each other and issuing pronouncements? There is no sense of urgency at 15 Beacon Street because there exists, by and large, no overwhelming pressure for good education. The motives operative in the third-floor meeting room include everything from office seeking to personal vanity, while the interest groups are, in one guise or another, merely the representatives of the system and its employees: the teachers' union, the Home and School Association (in reality a company-union PTA), the custodians, the administration, and, in the persons of Mrs. Hicks and O'Connor, the whole morass that makes the system indistinguishable from the interests of its own employees. With the exception of the growing number of Negroes who may, increasingly, become the concern of the state and federal governments, Boston simply lacks sufficient hostages to good education.

* * *

The administration, the School Committee, the teachers, the city's political and ethnic past, its geographical and political situation, its economy—all fit together to produce an attitude and a set of practices that keep the school system smoothly functioning and basically undisturbed. Except for an occasional example of a particularly odious political or personal situation (a former chairman sometimes fell asleep after a few too many drinks), the only thing that has recently shaken the system has been the imbalance fight. That battle, for better or worse, introduced a new political element into the old equilibrium. But the very thing that brought it on—civil rights—also helped obscure its educational consequences.

The 1965 election outcome changed few attitudes, and it has had virtually no impact on the system. Except for the hot breath of the state on the city's financial neck, the system, a year after the election, is probably the same as it was the year before. Arthur Gartland is gone from the School Committee, and because he is no longer there to exacerbate the battles that he inevitably lost, some people feel that the chances for genuine discussion of serious issues have slightly improved. The administration, under Ohrenberger's leadership, has made it somewhat easier for candidates outside Boston to take the city's teacher examinations: they are now given several times each year. (Boston is one of the few American systems that require such examinations; it requires them even of people with experience.) As a consequence the backgrounds and attitudes of entering teachers are slightly more diverse than those of the veterans: some now come from Tufts, Northeastern, Boston University, the University of Massachusetts, and other institutions not heretofore represented in large numbers. But there is no telling how many of the nonconformists will be selected out in the next few years; so far, at any rate, the recent procedural and administrative changes instituted by Ohrenberger have had little visible impact on the style of the system.

There has, however, been one important internal development, which occurred so quietly that it is rarely mentioned: a week after the 1965 School Committee election, on the night of the big East Coast power failure, the teachers of the system voted for representation by the American Federation of Teachers, and against the old, nationally unaffiliated Boston Teachers' Alliance. In choosing the more militant union, they started to establish what may be not only a source of countervailing power against the regular system but, perhaps more important, an agency of security that could, in the long run, offer serious competition to the hierarchical togetherness nurtured by the old establishment on Beacon Street. No one, of course, can be sure. Ultimately the union leadership may turn out to be simply a mirror image of the school hierarchy. Its major officers already include people like Fred Reilly, the brother of the former School Committee chairman, who are very much in the Beacon Street tradition and far more oriented to civil service than to trade unionism, let alone reform in education. And yet, the first showings of the union have been impressive. In its initial bargaining sessions with the School Committee, it secured increases in what is already an adequate, though hardly extravagant, teachers' salary scale, raising the maximum for people with a master's degree from $8,820 to $9,800, and the maximum for bachelors' degrees from $8,340 to $9,300. (Entering salaries of $5,460 and $5,940 changed hardly at all.) The union also won agreement on a pilot program of duty-free lunch periods for teachers and the hiring of teacher aides. (Boston loves trial programs, most of which demonstrate what has already been demonstrated under similar circumstances elsewhere, but which postpone a full commitment. Thus the system can put the change on the achievement list without really having to practice or pay for it.) Neither innovation affects many people and neither can be considered a major departure, but they do represent a start for the union. More important, the union list of specific complaints regarding the schools and teaching conditions indicates an awareness of school problems that no other critic of the system has fully articulated. If the Citizens for the Boston Schools had used the union material, they might have won more votes:

Discontinuance of the practice of keeping pupils out of classes for activities associated with recreation and entertainment.

The appointment of a committee to study modern methods of programming for language laboratories.

Limitation of the pupil load for (high school) English teachers to 100.

Immediate construction of an English High School building.

The organization of a remedial reading program for all schools.

Limitation on the size of the kindergarten and elementary classes to 25.

Assignment of guidance counselors to all junior high schools.

A duty-free lunch period for teachers.

A liberal sabbatical program.

The establishment of more special classes (classes for the handicapped and for slow learners).

The union also asked for better representation of teachers on existing curriculum development committees, the relief of teachers from clerical duties, the provision of adequate library facilities in all schools, the replacement of antiquated furniture, and the installation of adequate rest rooms. Of the remaining 150 items on the union's list—the list was part of the campaign material of the American Federation of Teachers in the 1965 bargaining election —some simply reflect the teachers' justified impatience with the endless administrative chores they must perform; others are petty; and still others stand no chance of being implemented in the near future, if at all. But the burden of the list places the union squarely on the side of better conditions for teaching as well as teachers, and against the going system. The tone of the program is honest in describing or alluding to problems that are educationally significant, in expressing a vague feeling that something is wrong— wrong with the procedures, wrong with morale, and wrong with education. One plank in the program states: "No supervisor may mark a group of candidates in any case where a relative of the supervisor is among the candidates." Another demands "democratic teachers' meetings with free and encouraged participation by all staff members." In some communities such demands would sound ludicrous, and even in Boston they may reflect paranoia as much as practice. And yet everyone knows that it helps to appear at School Committee meetings if one wants a promotion, that it is a good idea to "go around and get known." What makes the union demands significant in Boston is not their substance, but only the fact that someone had the temerity to make them.

* * *

Anyone who examines the system of the Boston schools finds it difficult to determine how much is Yankee skeleton and how much is Irish flesh. Through the years one very much helped shape the other. The administrators sometimes talk a bad clean-government rhetoric while playing a good, personal Irish game. Accuse them of too much Irishness and they throw back Yankee arrows.

The two mesh in a mutual conservatism. This is not to say that Boston is immune to change or innovation. The system is now fairly littered with demonstration projects and experiments, head starts, preschools, enrichments, compensatory programs, second chances, reading laboratories, summer reviews, pilot schools, team-teaching trials, and a whole host of other departures. It is developing, at least tentatively, and really for the first time, cooperative programs with Harvard, Northeastern, Boston University, and other colleges. It has a growing program of compensatory educa-

tion for culturally deprived children, and it is trying out or insti-
tuting new science and mathematics programs and new techniques
of teaching reading. Most of the innovation and planning—including the federally financed program of compensatory education—has been centered in a new Office of Program Development
(essentially a research and development staff) directed by an im-
port named Evans Clinchy. Clinchy, who had been associated with
Educational Services, Inc., an independent nonprofit organization
of curriculum developers, and with Educational Facilities Laboratory, a Ford Foundation offshoot concerned with academic archi-
tecture and equipment, is every inch an Ivy Leaguer, a crew-cut,
pipe-smoking six-foot-four-inch anomaly in a system administered by civil servants who have come up through the ranks. So
far, according to Ohrenberger, who proposed the office (which costs
the city not a dime) the transplant has been successful. Clinchy has
begun to build a staff, to plan a saturation project in a ghetto district, and, with varying degrees of success, to attempt to gain the
confidence of the administrators. Although it is still far too early
to see results, even from the compensatory program—which started long before 1965, when Clinchy was hired—he has established
himself as Boston's ambassador to Washington and Cambridge,
the man who can talk to the profs and the feds, and he represents
the brightest *internal* hope for innovation and change. He is bright,
competent, and probably not very well liked, even though his job
is established outside the hierarchy, giving him no foothold on any
ladder. To date the members of the School Committee have shown
little enthusiasm for his projects; by people like Mrs. Hicks, he is
sometimes treated as an interloper rather than an innovator, and she
is careful—and probably correct—to make sure he does not deprive
the system of its best classroom teachers for the purpose of staffing
his experiments. For the system as a whole, the great hope—or the
great threat—is that he will make federal money so indispensable,
and that he will create so many jobs, as to make the Office of Program Development politically unassailable, and perhaps even academically effective.

But so far, the system's long list of changes—many of them initiated under Ohrenberger's direction—has had almost no effect
on educational substance for most of the children most of the time.
Many of the innovations affect only a handful of pupils—a school

there, a few classes there—and there has been little carryover to regular practices, either in program or in attitude. The innovations tend to remain well encapsulated, like droplets of oil on still water. While the system proudly publishes the list of special ventures, individual administrators complain that everything is moving too fast, that they do not have time to plan, or even to think. At bottom, most of them simply don't know how to run the system their way *and* to make changes at the same time. They are genuinely confused about the avalanche of new demands being made upon them and upon American education generally. They have, they feel, always given Negroes equal treatment; why suddenly are there so many complaints? They have always run the system smoothly and honestly; why suddenly are there so many critics? Their defensiveness is neither malicious nor cynical. It is the defensiveness of decent, honest men caught in a revolution they did not make, don't understand, and in which they want no part.

From the very top to somewhere near the very bottom, the Boston system is steeped in conservative ideas and traditional practices, in a patronizing outlook, and in subtle prejudice. Its leaders look upon themselves as caretakers. "Every day," one of the administrators told a Catholic newspaper reporter, "I say novenas for the Negro children. The Holy Spirit is right here, with me, telling me to look out for those poor children." Among the staff—teachers and administrators—are hundreds of competent, concerned people, people with a genuine feeling for the children they teach and counsel. But their style, almost invariably, is the same. Despite new demands and ideas, despite the attacks of the Citizens for the Boston Schools, the editorials in the newspapers, the political campaigns, and the not-always-subtle criticisms of the Catholic hierarchy itself, that style remains unaffected. "The example of the parochial schools carries over and the Cardinal's statements about segregation do not," said one Catholic critic. "They were nurtured in the first, but they don't pay much attention to Cushing because they feel his liberal pronouncements carry no authority, that he is meddling in things that aren't his business. People in this city are pretty patronizing about the Church anyhow. You should hear those references to someone as 'a good little priest' or the way Bill O'Connor at the School Committee talks about 'the good nuns.' The administrators respond to authority. They know how to obey.

But only to people in the system, to people who have authority, and who can use it."

The Boston system, like every other school organization, has its internal harmony; what makes it so perpetual is that the forces of change remain outside. The School Committee, the administration, the majority of the teachers, and the electorate reinforce each other. Programs and attitudes follow what the administration senses to be the wishes of the community, and especially of its politically vocal elements. "The professionals," said a Negro leader in the South End, "have no convictions. If the Negroes constituted the majority they might be on our side. This all-Catholic administration is about as un-Christian as anything you can find, a good reflection of the prevalent Catholic attitude in Boston. No one on Beacon Street pays any attention to the Cardinal or to anyone else because they're considered outsiders . . . You know, they haven't really made it, the Irish. They haven't made it as *class*. If they had, they'd be willing to help someone else. There is so much that could be done here. But most people in Boston aren't interested in educational issues, are not interested in improving the schools, and so the administration isn't either." That criticism was made in the bitter days after the 1965 election, when it seemed that nothing could be done to alter the system. It is unnecessarily harsh, and perhaps not entirely accurate since, even with a change in electoral attitude, the internal traditions and relationships—inherited from decades of practice—would tend to perpetuate themselves. There is, furthermore, a considerable amount of dedication and conviction, even within the precincts of Beacon Street. Ohrenberger and many members of his staff are not clock watchers, while many teachers and administrators give a great deal of extra time and energy to a job that is, by its very nature, and even under the best of circumstances, frustrating and thankless. But even at its best—and that can be reasonably good—the Boston system is rarely anything but antiquated and often obsolescent. With a style developed by Puritanical Yankees, reinforced and amplified by an equally Puritanical church and parochial schools, and honed to precision by Irish civil servants, one could hardly expect it to be anything else.

THE CITY of Boston operates 15 senior high schools, 18 junior highs, and 160 elementary schools, a quarter of them predominantly Negro, and many of them erected well before the people who now staff them were born. Among these establishments are two trade schools, three academically selective high schools oriented toward college preparation, and a variety of district schools, many of them so overcrowded that they have simply become spaces occupied by bodies trying to survive discomfort, and not educational facilities at all. In some, teachers try to conduct classes jammed with 45 children; in others they must operate in the basement, or in temporarily converted auditoriums and lunchrooms. Few of the junior high schools have libraries, and the elementary schools have none. Many of the texts are outdated, torn, dirty, and, often, when they are modern, there are not enough to go around. At one predominantly Negro school a high-ranking administration official told complaining parents that textbooks were not really necessary as long as a teacher was in the classroom.

Each year the children who attend these schools fall farther behind national norms in reading and arithmetic. In the second grade Boston children read about five months above grade. By the sixth grade they are four months behind and Negro children are almost a year behind (by contrast, the average sixth grader in New York is four months ahead); by the time they are in the tenth grade they rank in the bottom third in national tests (that is, the average Boston school pupil falls into the 35th precentile in reading; the 50th percentile is "average"). Concurrently the Boston mean in arithmetic falls at the 37th percentile. Until recently there were no remedial reading programs in the junior high schools.

Two thirds of the Boston teaching force is composed of women, one fourth are more than 55 years old, and ninety-nine percent are white. (One fourth of the children are Negro.) The quality of their teaching varies, as it does everywhere else. Some talk about "process-centered" learning, about team teaching, and ungraded classes. Some are using modern mathematics and the new programs developed by the Physical Sciences Study Committee (PSSC) and the Biological Sciences Curriculum Study (BSCS). But for the most part they operate with methods and outlooks that have been passed from generation to generation by people still convinced that the quality of education in Boston has continued undiminished since the glorious days over a century ago when Horace Mann, the educational reformer, described the Massachusetts schools as "a system of unsurpassable grandeur and efficiency." Some of the buildings date from that era—and so, indeed, do the styles of instruction. And both have suffered, and survived, the ravages of time. Teaching in Boston can still be very good; but good or bad, it is almost invariably old-fashioned.

Boston's 4,000 teachers, its 96,000 schoolchildren, and its various programs and facilities comprise a system that bears the sociological and cultural marks of an older America: a faith in fundamental rote instruction, in character and discipline, in good order and decent manners. It resembles one of those faintly brown photographs of immigrants arriving at Ellis Island, or of Warren G. Harding making the first presidential radio address. One can get nostalgic about the Boston schools with their dirty red walls and their Gothic roofs, their Spartan asphalt playgrounds, their dark halls and disinfected stairways. One can be charmed at the sight of thirty pupils rising en masse as the principal enters the classroom, saying "Good morning, children," and at their echoing response, "Good morning, Miss O'Brien." One can even become bemused as a junior high school principal, watching the files of children passing in the hall, stops a boy to ask, stridently, "Where's your necktie?" To visit these schools, and to hear their teachers and principals, is to return to an older version of democracy that presumes, for example, that equal opportunity in education can eradicate inequality in prior social or economic status, that any deprived group can surmount obstacles by its own efforts, and that the Horatio Alger virtues are the keys to success. A teacher asserts proudly that all the children—black and white—get along fine in her class, that she sees no reason for "all this friction between the races." A high school student declares that in his school no one cares about the religion of any other individual. A principal asserts that if all those underprivileged kids would just be willing to do a decent day's work they'd get ahead just like every other minority in America. Over a cup of coffee an administrator confesses—and this one hears again and again—that there was no trouble in his school until the civil rights boycotts started. It was then that the children began to complain, to make demands about new textbooks, and to cause difficulties for the teachers, the truant officers, and the principal.

One can begin to believe in the inherent logic of this world, a world where all people are treated equally, no matter what the color of their skin, no matter what their political beliefs or their economic background. But then, invariably, one is reminded that this is not a play, a charade, a book of old snapshots. One is reminded that there is discrimination and deprivation and that they combine to make life very much unequal. One is reminded that the education Boston offers is real, that it is happening now, in this place at this time. It presumes to be education for *this* world—for the twentieth and even the twenty-first century—for a culture of process, where change is the only constant, where all "facts" are perishable, and where education (not ward politics or family ties or even "character") is the prime condition for survival. One hears terribly little about dealing with the problems generated by that sort of culture. The frustrating business of providing relevant education to lower-middle-class kids who have only a dim and tenuous connection with the official world of success—if any—is one of the least discussed subjects in Boston, and one of the most pressing. Forty-six of Boston's 200-odd schools are over 50 percent Negro, 21 percent are 90 percent Negro (many, of course, are 100 percent white), and each year the blight of *de facto* segregation spreads. The Negro schools are among the oldest in the city, many of them dating to the turn of the century; a few have been described simply as "Civil War jobs." Following the common pattern, the

Negro schools register lowest in reading scores and other tests of educational achievement—and the more Negro they are, the lower they rank—and they display the most severe signs of educational and social trauma—higher dropout rates, higher truancy figures, and, apparently, higher rates of teacher turnover. But the problems of the Negro schools, which Boston shares with every other major city, are only a reflection of the educational liabilities that plague the Boston schools generally and that, despite their critics, they seem unwilling or unable to overcome. Boston's deprived include middle-class Jews and working-class Irish; Negroes have no corner on deprivation. Indeed, in a system like Boston's, almost every child is deprived. More than most cities, Boston tends to look backward for solutions to new problems. Its education faces the rear.

*　*　*

The pride, the penultimate, the model of the Boston system is still the Latin School, now well into its fourth century. "If it's nothing," said Wilfred Leo O'Leary, its headmaster, "the rest is nothing"; and although Latin is in many respects unique, a separate ward within the public school establishment, one can hardly understand the rest without visiting it. *This* is the bridge between the Yankee tradition and contemporary Boston, the link between Puritans and Irish Catholics, between all that is classical and traditional and whatever is modern about Boston education. The Latin School gives Boston more to brag about than all the rest of the system put together. Its graduates and students earn the vast bulk of the city's academic distinctions, represent one third of its college admissions (almost half the boys) and virtually all its national scholastic honors. It is the Latin School that ties the city system to its history, gives it its standards and the limited glory it enjoys, and provides its most competent high school teaching. Because the Latin School is Boston's pride, its ensign of excellence, it tends to stamp upon all the city its patterns of classical rigidity—patterns which, because of the Latin School, are inevitably associated with quality. Part of Boston's tragedy is that its greatest model is three hundred years old. It lacks anything new to follow; thus all of the system is still trying to become what Latin was a century ago. According to Headmaster O'Leary (all Boston high school principals are called headmasters), the Latin School is not an institution, it is a state of mind. O'Leary is himself a graduate of the school, much as one would expect the president of Harvard to be an alumnus of his institution—a personable Irishman whose primary commitment is to his school and not to the bureaucrats downtown. A former Air Corps lieutenant colonel—a not uncommon background for high school principals—O'Leary mixes a liberal Catholicism (including a subtle disdain for the authoritarianism of the parochial schools) with a profound respect for academic order and discipline, a gentle passion for the teachers' union, and a fierce possessive pride in his school and in the possibilities it represents. As O'Leary shows the visitor through the building he loses few opportunities to recall the traditions and history of this, the oldest educational establishment in English North America. Founded in 1635, Boston Latin fairly oozes with the names of great men. Its first headmaster was among the religious dissenters expelled from Massachusetts Bay Colony with Anne Hutchinson; five of its alumni signed the Declaration of Independence, among them John Hancock, Sam Adams, Benjamin Franklin, and Robert Treat Paine; one became the architect of the White House, several served as president of Harvard, and one, Leonard Bernstein, is now probably the best-known orchestral conductor in the United States. Around the walls of the auditorium are the names of other alumni—Henry Knox, Edward Everett, Ralph Waldo Emerson, Charles Sumner, Wendell Phillips, Phillips Brooks, Henry Lee Higginson, George Santayana—and in the corridors and the administrative offices are the plaques, the scrolls, the pictures, and memorabilia recalling—not last year's football victories, although those are also remembered—but names and events in Yankee history that go back to the very roots of the Massachusetts Bay Colony.

The Latin School, located in a forty-year-old classic-revival building near the Harvard Medical School, and surrounded by other educational and medical institutions, draws its students from all parts of the city. (Most Boston students attend neighborhood or district high schools; Latin, Girls Latin, English High, and Boston Technical High School select their students by competitive examination.) At Latin everyone is prepping for college—and everyone eventually goes—not only for the customary suburban status reason, but because success means economic advancement. (The school calls itself "breeder of democracy"—a funnel through which able and ambitious boys from Boston can negotiate the bottleneck of academic selectivity and social opportunity.) For the students, many of them now from working-class families, the pressure is phenomenal; this is the best opportunity they will ever have. "It's push, push, push," said a senior. Thus there are no discipline problems—transgressors can always be sentenced back to their district schools—and no one complains about the fact that at Latin quality and high standards mean rigor, structure, discipline, and hard work. This is not a freewheeling intellectual market place buzzing with ideas and activism. It is a hardworking factory inhabited by competent people looking for a place in the sun. Latin does not pretend that it is doing anything other than preparing students to get into college—that is, to *pass tests*. There is little nonsense about indulging in the life of the mind. Just pass tests. Thus three hours of homework per night and no deviation. Overwhelmed by the Emersons, the Brookses, and the Adamses on the one hand, and by parental pressure and college ambitions on the other, the 2,000 boys at Latin are in many respects far more reminiscent of those at a staid and somewhat grim private academy than those at a public high school. "The school's primary function was to force the student to keep busy for a few hours daily," said a recent alumnus. "Whether or not he was thinking seemed to be of no concern to anybody."

Because of its reputation, the Latin School operates like a quasi-independent barony within a feudal structure—a special ward with a powerful constituency, a scholarship endowment close to $500,000, an uninterrupted relationship with Harvard, and an alumni body sufficiently enthusiastic and well enough organized that it can still make itself heard downtown. A decade ago, when its membership decided that "the place had become a dumping ground for people who couldn't teach anywhere else" the association met with the administration and School Committee, exercising enough pressure to raise admission standards, to remove some thirty temporary teachers from the faculty, and, eventually, to get O'Leary appointed principal. Now O'Leary, who sometimes speaks of the school like an old New England Headmaster, and sometimes like a ward boss, hopes to raise his scholarship endowment to $1 million, to find still better teachers, through, among other things, a process he calls cannibalism, and to build new classrooms and a new library. "I'm going to see the Mayor," he said, "and I'll tell him that if he gets us the new library I'll name it after him." (The Latin School Library was locked from January to October 1966 because there was no replacement for the librarian, who had died early in the year.)

Despite O'Leary's efforts, despite the pressure of the alumni, Latin survives as much on reputation and selectivity as on academic drive and intellectual vitality. When the classical tradition began to wane in Boston, and the old Yankees were replaced by Irish civil servants, little was added in the way of new ideas and almost nothing in reform. Classical rigidity and impartiality were supplanted by genial politicians who, inevitably, helped link change with decline, not with innovation. Thus many of the most earnest defenders of Latin—men who knew the school when three fourths of its graduates went to Harvard—associate challenges to rigidity with political favoritism and corruption. A decade ago, Philip Marson, one of the great Latin School masters, published a blistering description of Latin after the politicians captured the system and the processes of selection and promotion:

> Not only were the victims of this "merit" system subjected to innumerable indignities; they had no appeal from the verdict after the rating lists were published. The figures were rigged so cleverly that exposure of their falsity and the chicanery underlying them became impossible. A visiting supervisor might spend only ten minutes in a classroom before passing judgment. He might, as in the case of one of the greatest teachers we ever had in the school, grade him so low for a piece of scrap paper dropped on the floor by a careless boy that the poor man was put out of the running. (Incidentally, this outraged scholar and gentleman refused ever to be rated again.) Or the visitor might have had an unpleasant incident just before his visitation and is in a venomous mood as he enters the classroom of the ill-fated victim. But even if these possibilities are ignored, the candidate is still faced with the final reckoning at the judgment seat.
>
> As it works out, no dirty work can be proved and no outcry is therefore in order. If one finds, as I did in each of the four times I was rated, that he has been accredited with well over nine hundred points of a possible thousand, he has apparently no cause for complaint. After all, no human being should believe that he can attain perfection; and if, as in 1940, I was

awarded fourth place among thirty-five candidates with 917 points—just one point below the man ahead of me, I should surely be happy about or at least resigned to the outcome. Normally only one or two positions were available during the three-year period during which the list was in effect; and invariably, when the new one appeared, for some strange but not incomprehensible reason, three or four names—up to that time unknown or unimpressive—suddenly appeared at the summit. The only rational explanation of such magic was that these nonpareils had certain intangible qualities which became visible during the intervening three-year period and which deserved recognition by the Board of Superintendents and the School Committee. What they were we rarely discovered; and when we did, it was obvious that they varied with the candidate. He might, as in one case, belong in the same parish as the assistant superintendent who visited him. This man was given poor marks until one Sunday when the omniscient official discovered that his assumption that the candidate was a Protestant was wrong. The next rating enabled him to go ahead. Doubts as to the validity of this implication may be dispelled by noting the roster of high-ranking administrators: the conclusion is inevitable that to be promoted, a man might not have to be a graduate of either Boston College or Holy Cross, but it would certainly help. By 1954, the superintendent, his five assistants, all supervisors, and all high school headmasters except one (Kelley of Tufts) possessed this helpful qualification. No Protestant or Jewish candidate during the preceding twenty-five years seems to have been able to overcome the handicap of being an alumnus of Harvard, M.I.T., Tufts, or other "inferior" institutions. Objective evaluation had little to do with where one landed on the list.

This perversion of what had begun as a merit system had devastating effects on the morale of the men, who depended upon promotion for increases in salary. Disillusionment, despair, and bitterness appeared and affected their attitudes and, finally, their work. Until the pinch of poverty or the itch for power disturbed a good teacher, he was happy in his work and contented to remain at his post. Many men who had observed the workings of the system refused to be browbeaten into taking courses, to be subservient or acquiescent, or to be subjected to unpleasant extra duties. They either did not present themselves for rating or ran the gauntlet only once and ignored it thereafter. Usually these insurgents had outside sources of income or fewer obligations and hence refused to submit to the rigmarole of accumulated credits, meaningless visitations, or incidental indignities.

The effects on the school system were many when objectivity gave way to political maneuvering. We had witnessed a striking change while the free-wheeling James Michael Curley was mayor. Not only had City Hall become a bargaining center for hundreds of plums distributed to the faithful, but even School Headquarters—until about 1920 a sacrosanct and inviolable sanctuary of incorruptible men—had become a replica of the noisome political swamp down the hill on School Street. The climax came when widespread scandals connected with job-selling and favoritism were publicized. Later the rated lists came under scrutiny when a disappointed but capable candidate for headmaster exposed the workings of the system. Among other things, he pointed out that a comparatively unknown newcomer had jumped in one rating from the bottom of the list to the top, leaping over some twenty-eight candidates who were ahead of him. With such goings-on, the schools were sure to feel the effects.

At Latin School we felt the impact almost immediately. Heads of department appeared who were unschooled and ineffective. In only a few accidental instances were they qualified; and in several cases, large staffs were headed by mediocrities who were outclassed in scholarship, pedagogical skill, and executive ability by four or more men under them. In the early years of my tenure, the momentum furnished by the traditional standards of the school sustained us; but when one headmaster, during the last five years of his term, refused to fight, the end of qualitative work was assured.

* * *

The evidence of the constantly deteriorating standards of achievement and grading in the elementary schools had become so overwhelming that successive headmasters of our school had protested. Their just claims, however, brought no change in the admission requirements; for neither the school committee nor the board of superintendents would consent to the recommendations proposed. In the past the restrictions consisted of the simple device of demanding that the candidate have marks of A or B in four major subjects during his sixth-grade or eighth-grade year—that is, in English, geography, history, and mathematics; and it had served fairly well to weed out the wholly unqualified. (It was possible for a boy who had grades below this level to gain admittance by passing examinations.) When, however, it became apparent to the faculty that (a) little had been taught or learned before arrival at our doors and (b) dependence on the marks donated by kind teachers had become worse than useless, our head was prevailed upon to petition that students thereafter be admitted by examination only. But we got nowhere, partly because some people presented specious arguments that such a method would be undemocratic, some feared political consequences inflicted by voters whose sons might fail, but most of those in control were either indifferent to our plight or incapable of seeing the problem. We were not surprised at the refusal to give serious consideration to our request; for few, if any, of those who would decide the matter were qualified, either by education or interests, to pass fair judgment, even if they had wished to. They consisted largely of political hacks ambitious for greater power or privilege. But for a long period of years we had at least one member who tried to perform his civic duty creditably. Unfortunately, despite his good intentions, he was regularly outvoted four-to-one.

With a school committee made up, for the most part, of well-meaning fools or scheming politicians, the teachers of the city could scarcely be expected to be bubbling over with confidence and hope that help for the ailing schools would come from that source. Neither could they count on appointments that were within the Committee's jurisdiction or subject to its sanction to reflect sound judgment. The result was inevitable. With rare exceptions, the administrators and the headmasters were conformists, unoriginal mediocrities, congenial joiners who belonged to the right organizations or who managed to be seen at every important wake, and invariably compromisers trying to perpetuate and protect the escalator system. The system was, as a matter of fact, self-perpetuating; for no man who hoped for promotion dared to cross his immediate superior or indicate disapproval of any aspect of the way the schools were operated. It was a rare man, indeed, who could afford the luxury of originality, intellectual vigor, political independence, religious deviation, or educational non-conformity.

Latin has been considerably restored since the decline that Marson describes. The alumni themselves were largely responsible for that restoration; new and more competent teachers have been brought in, admissions standards tightened, and competitive examinations instituted. But the restoration did not move Latin ahead; it moved it back, back toward its history and tradition, not toward innovation and experimentation. "We're willing to try anything," said O'Leary. "We're using the new mathematics and the new physics. But I think the pendulum is swinging the other way, back to the older approach. In math you've got to have answers."

In a ninth grade English class, the students are reading works from a standard anthology of poetry edited by Louis Untermeyer. The teacher, a red-haired young man with glasses, was recruited by O'Leary from a tough junior high school. ("I want men from gray areas who don't show intolerance with a slow boy," O'Leary said. "I want my teachers to have determination. These kids here are so bright that they'll take right off with a little guidance. All you have to do is correlate the classes with the College Board results; then you can find out who's teaching.") The students all wear ties, sitting in straight rows before the instructor. The room, with its faded green walls and worn wood floor, gives the appearance of having been subject to a timeless stream of students now happily and successfully elsewhere, a basic training camp which leads to better things. From the windows one can see some of the towers of the city—the promised world, the enchanted castles, of the academic fairy tale.

The poem under discussion at this moment is by Alan Seeger, a young American who was killed in World War I. It is called "I Have a Rendezvous with Death" and it is not a very appealing piece of verse. Sentimental and prosaic, it falls into that large abyss of works that educators decree as appropriate for students, but which no other human being has read for years.

> I have a rendezvous with Death
> At some disputed barricade,
> When Spring comes back with rustling shade
> And apple-blossoms fill the air—

I have a rendezvous with Death
When Spring brings back blue days and fair.

It may be he shall take my hand
And lead me into his dark land
And close my eyes and quench my breath—
It may be I shall pass him still.
I have a rendezvous with Death
On some scarred slope of battered hill,
When Spring comes round again this year
And the first meadow-flowers appear.

God knows 'twere better to be deep
Pillowed in silk and scented down,
Where Love throbs out in blissful sleep,
Pulse nigh to pulse, and breath to breath,
Where hushed awakenings are dear, . . .
But I've a rendezvous with Death
At midnight in some flaming town,
When Spring trips north again this year,
And I to my pledged word am true,
I shall not fail that rendezvous.

"Now," says the red-haired teacher, "what does rendezvous mean?"

    A. (The boy stands up, as required.) It means a meeting.

    Q. When does this take place?

    A. In the Spring?

    Q. Is that when it takes place?

    A. In a war.

    Q. How does he treat death in these lines?

    A. Like a person.

    Q. What do you call that?

    A. Personification.

    Q. What is a disputed barricade?

    A. It's an obstacle.

    Q. The language in this poem is suggestive of something taking place. What is it saying?

    A. He's saying there's no chance to escape it.

    Q. Why does he think he'll get killed?

(Some confusion ensues, a few bad guesses, then the teacher writes on the board. "War is something which is personal.")

    Q. What was his purpose in writing a poem like this?

A. He's speaking out against . . .
Q. Against what?
A. Against the fear of death.
Q. Against cowardice? . . .
A. Against war? . . .
A. He's saying some people don't realize the true meaning of death in war . . .

The class moves to another selection of verse, a part of the "Rhyme of the Ancient Mariner," then to William Cullen Bryant's "To a Waterfowl" (Q. "Who can tell me what the abyss of heaven is?"). And then to still another selection. The questions are short and factual, demanding meaning and explanation, rarely urging discussion or suggesting the pleasure of the verse. The operation is one of fact-finding, of "doing" the literature, competently, desperately, methodically. These poets are gray, ghostly men, and their works are discussed like riddles or mathematics problems for which one must find a specific answer. They are exercises. Nothing about them seems very real—the irony or the joy, the ideas, the imagery, or the verse. All that really exists is the duty of deciphering, of understanding words and phrases, of achieving answers and making it through to the next, and then the next, and the next.

In another room with the same green walls, the same brown woodwork, a history teacher—a Negro—is discussing Napoleon with an Advanced Placement class of seniors, among them some of the brightest students in the school. If they do well on the Advanced Placement test they may be excused from an introductory college course, and this class, this year, is designed to prepare them for that test.

Q. What is Italy good for as far as Napoleon is concerned?
A. (As in the other classes, the boys stand to answer, a requirement suitable for formal debate but fatal to free-flowing discussion.) It's a place where he can put his relative in office.
Q. He is a good family man. What did he get in Italy?
A. Art works.
Q. Yes, he is a good art critic. He gets the Mona Lisa. He picks up no trash . . . Why do the Italian young men join his army? Why do they march to Moscow? Is it because Russia is a great threat to Naples?

A. He drafts them? . . .

A. Sir, the Italians volunteered. In the Army, positions were awarded on merit; there was no favoritism . . .

Q. He said, "Look at me, I'm a dark man and my name is Bonaparte. I'm really Italian." The Italians are so overjoyed; they want to have a Napoleon relative as king . . . You still haven't told me whether you thought Napoleon was a great man.

A. He was a great man because he got his way.

A. He accomplished what he wanted to accomplish.

Q. Suppose I make up my mind to foul up this class and flunk all of you. Does that make me a great man?

There is fun in the teacher's voice, perhaps more than in those of the students. He suggests that there may be pleasure in this work, and that the plaster figures of history were once human. But the syllabus, imposed by the necessity to pass a test, does not permit much play; it demands no inductive thought, insisting rather on factual coverage of five centuries of European history:

Who were the leading personalities of the Congress of Vienna and what were their immediate and long term objectives?

Examine the disaffection between the Dual Monarchy and her subject nationalities.

Examine the underlying causes of World War II as they related to the post-Versailles period.

Some of the practices of the Latin School have changed in recent years. "Everything used to be parse, parse, parse," a teacher reported with some pride and amusement. "How those old Yankees made people work." Until recently the school offered no social science in the sophomore and junior years and no biology at all. It prescribed Latin, English, mathematics, history, and certain sciences. Now there are a few more electives and somewhat more flexibility in programs and learning styles (there is, for example, a language laboratory). But Latin still offers no history other than American, European, and world, no Russian or Spanish, no economics or sociology, no music or art. Its bookstore, which sells about $100 worth of paperbacks a week (to 2,000 boys, for an average sale of under $2 per student per year) is pathetically understocked, underutilized and, underpromoted. Although Latin's stu-

87

dents report serious discussions in their free time—mostly at lunch —the evidence of intellectual interest is meager. "Today we talked about the Missouri Compromise in class," one said, "and then we talked about it right through lunch—you know, did the North or the South compromise, that kind of question." All of them feel they must read outside, mainly to keep up with the competition and the assignments, but few of them read very much. Where students in the better suburban schools go from class to class with the most unexpected volumes under their arms, the stacks under the arms of the Latin students are composed of the drab covers of fading texts, adorned occasionally by a pocket dictionary or a paper edition of *Faust*, assigned by a German teacher.

What remains of the old Latin School is not its intellectualism but its concern for patriotism, character, and morality. The school, like the rest of the city, has suffered from the exodus of the middle class. Once there was a liberal mixture of middle-class kids, sons of doctors from Dorchester, of Jewish lawyers from Brighton, or of South End businessmen. Recently there has been a growing proportion of boys from working-class families, more children of broken homes, more representatives of families just getting on the first rung of gentility. (There are, however, virtually no Negroes.) "Our biggest job here now," said O'Leary, "is the inculcation of ideals. What I want is the strong middle-of-the-roaders, those are the kids who get the job done. The trouble with people who find things too easy is that they sometimes quit when they run into real obstacles. I want to produce men who are willing to defend the ramparts . . . Too many people have acquisitive values these days, not cultural values. You know where the great American desert lies? It lies under his hat."

* * *

The city's other public schools reflect the Latin style, if not its quality. Because of the attraction of the selective public institutions, the district or neighborhood high schools are deprived of the best of the city's remaining talent. (Many students who fail to be admitted to Latin, or who flunk out, attend parochial or, if they can, suburban high schools. The Latin School's prime competitor is the Catholic Boston College High.) While the various neighborhood high schools offer some specialized programs, with each school claiming to concentrate in some special area—music and art in one, auto mechanics in another, business education in another, agriculture in still another—their vocational programs, even when they are oriented to contemporary trades and techniques, rarely prepare students for the continuing requirements of retraining in the years ahead. Their graduates learn to deal with certain pieces of equipment—arc-welding machines, the drill press, the shaper or milling machine—but they are rarely equipped, academically or intellectually, to continue learning through a lifetime during which not only the equipment but even the trade may become obsolete, and during which every individual must expect to change not only jobs but careers. The academic staple in the high schools remains routine instruction in English, history, mathematics, and science, instruction rarely oriented to the requirements of their students and almost never rooted in significant intellectual or social questions. Most of their courses seem to operate on the assumption that their students will go to college, although in fact almost none of them does. Of the 4,454 Boston high school graduates in 1964 (the latest year for which figures are available) 1,121—about one fourth —went to degree-granting colleges. Of these 1,121 almost 700 were graduates of the two Latin Schools and Boston Technical High. South Boston High School sent seven percent of its graduates to college; Jamaica Plain High sent eight percent; Hyde Park High eleven percent; Charlestown High four percent. (Despite Jamaica Plain's courses in agriculture, incidentally, no Boston graduate went into farming.)

And yet, everywhere they play the game of college. At Dorchester High, which sends six percent of its graduates to degree-granting colleges, a large proportion of the students are enrolled in the "college program" because, as one of them said, "high school isn't enough anymore. Everything is computers and IBM." At the same time, because many students work—often as department store clerks—they do little homework and no independent reading or study. A few of them, as seniors, resent their lack of preparation—although that resentment is usually turned on the junior high schools. "It's stupid to be doing grammar as a senior in high school," said a student. "We should be reading plays. But my junior high teacher never made us work. He talked about TV all the time; it was fun, but I didn't learn any English."

Learning English, or learning anything else, means recitation, memorization, and drill. The official curriculum guides treat teachers as simpleminded clerks, and students as data-ingestors. They reduce understanding to outlines and "suggestions to teachers," learning to gimmicks ("students will be interested in 'bulls' —'u' means to buy—and in 'bears'—'e' means to sell"), and education to superficialities. They deal in clichés and pieties, and in the tired liturgy of obsolete Americanisms:

Markets for real selling are destroyed by subsidies.
Subsidies tend to stifle initiative.

Emphasize the growing popularity of the outboard motor.

Mass production, the pursuit of pleasure, the demand for luxuries, the worship of efficiency, the scorn for idealism, and an open disregard for law characterized the "mad decade" of the 1920s.

The Congress under the Articles of Confederation was powerless to prevent political and economic disorders.

The annexation of Texas and the dispute over the Texan boundary were important causes of the Mexican war.

By their nature—and by their intent, which minimizes the negative and the unpleasant in American life—they exclude the possibilities of qualification, complexity, and richness, the dynamic energy of controversy and ambiguity. There is no suggestion, for example, that the Mexican War was regarded as an imperialistic war, and that it led to America's greatest act of civil disobedience, that the 1920s were also characterized by the last loud gasp of rural morality, by native intolerance, and by an outpouring of official cant, and that subsidies have very significant and accepted social functions necessary to the creation or restoration of initiative. The collective voice of the curriculum writers—usually an *ad hoc* committee of Boston teachers and principals—is the passive voice of the index card. It assumes the data of history or economics to be static, pre-ordained, ever-existing wisdom lying around in textbooks and classrooms ready for consumption and regurgitation. It regards understanding as limited, closed, and subject to outlines, lists of activities, terms to know, persons to identify, places to locate, and, simply, events. It treats the life of the classroom as a constant one-way flow and it regards the function of the social sciences—and other fields as well—to be a series of moral and cultural precepts urging loyalty and respect for the established order. More than anything else it exudes disrespect for the intelligence of children, committing them to an endless series of formalities validated only by the standards of the system itself. In a high school English class the students are reminded that "Saturday the College Board takes place. I'm tuning you up . . . Now who is the next reciter?" and in another the teacher proudly asserts that her class is based on "drill and more drill." There are somnambulent recitations about the Zimmerman telegram, the Treaty of Brest-Litovsk, and the Triple Entente (or was it the Triple Alliance? . . . Now who belonged to it? . . . and what did the Sussex Pledge pledge?). In a government class the teacher writes on the board:

I. Democracy—government by consent of the people
    A. Freedom to criticize
    (Teacher, as she writes: "We certainly have that in this country; think of the draft card burners and all those protest marchers.")
    B. Government exists for the people as opposed to totalitarian government where people exist for state

II. Authoritarianism—Government by single leader or group
    A. Permits private ownership of property
    B. Restricts political action and freedom of expression

(Teacher, aside again: "There'd be no criticism of the government in this country if we had a totalitarian system." Is she pleased or not? Perhaps she feels that the protests are the price she has to pay in order to make the claim of democracy defensible.) Now she puts a long chart on the board, headed "Secretariat." For thirty minutes the chalk scratches out the constitutional structure of the Soviet system while, behind her, blue ball points and stubby pencils copy what she writes. As the chalk flows across the board there are more asides: "The Soviet Union's space achievements have been made at the expense of the people . . . It's true that the Russians have put up a lot of housing lately, but the buildings are so shoddy that they have to put nets outside to catch the falling bricks . . . Russia is not a classless society; there are special stores for government officials . . ." The pencils follow sluggishly behind. "The All Union Congress is elected by the local communist parties . . ." In the corner of the board someone has written "eight days left for seniors."

* * *

The pride of the district high schools is cleanliness, order, and character, and none is easily achieved. "We're very crowded here," says the principal of one. "We can't turn anyone down; we can never say 'no more.' But my halls and lunchroom are always clean. This year they gave me new lockers for the boys, and that was a big help." On the wall hangs a sign certifying that the school recently won honorable mention in a campaign to curb vandalism. In another school the principal explains that keeping boys and girls separate in the lunchroom helps maintain order, that "we like to let them know we're watching their conduct and attendance." "There is no rule requiring boys to wear ties," he says, "but those who don't have to come in at 8:15 in the morning." One principal concedes that his greatest concern is that the students who come from the junior high schools can't read, that it's hard to get them to study, that many are just there to receive a diploma. But he is an exception. For many, if not most, the big problems are simply an avalanche of little ones: to move all the students in and out of the auditorium quickly, to avoid crowding in the halls, to make certain that the lunchroom is patrolled, that the proper reports are sent downtown, that the honor certificates are awarded, that substitutes appear for absent teachers and all classes are "covered," that the rooms are tidy, that school, despite the crowding, despite a faulty boiler and some doubtful pipes, despite some problem kids, despite inadequate materials—that despite all these things, school opens on time each morning and closes on time each afternoon. The real headache in this desperately superannuated system is just to keep the thing going at all.

The students are honest, dutiful, and curiously moralistic. Most of them are from working-class families; few of them represent homes where much is read, where major issues are debated, or where the nature of the world is subject to a great deal of question. In schools like Dorchester High they come from the most polyglot ethnic backgrounds—Irish, Italian, Polish, Greek, Negro. The older teachers recall the days when Dorchester was predominantly Jewish, when motivation and competition were more intense, and when more could be assumed about basic skills. Now the students represent a population that has already been doubly screened out—screened out by the loss of middle-class children, and screened out by the selectivity of the Latin Schools. And yet, strangely, they strike one as more competent, more sage, more mature than one would suspect. They are neither anxious nor depressed (nor are they in any way rebellious). Rather they appear to be cheerful, obedient, and thoroughly decent. Like their teachers, they see education as something important and—if it is to be good —as vaguely repressive. It rarely occurs to them—and then only to a few—that learning can be intellectually stimulating or exciting. The boys regard the universal requirement to wear ties as simply another aspect of their preparation ("You have to get used to it when you get out into business"), and they admire the principal's tolerance in allowing the school's teen-age professional musicians to wear Beatle haircuts. They speak about marks and teachers and cars, but they never become involved in civil rights or political activism, never talk about foreign policy, even though many face the draft, never discuss religion, and rarely say anything that suggests that they view their own education as inadequate. None of these things seems to affect them very much. To ask them about civil rights is almost like asking them if they're interested in the geology of the moon. They are not really concerned, and are not bothered by their own indifference. Many of them are proud of their good behavior in the school and at its social affairs. The best of them view their own world and their education much in the same way as their teachers and administrators. For them school is analogous to their work at Filene's and Grant's: it is a job, it is necessary, and it is unquestioned.

* * *

The Oliver Wendell Holmes Junior High School, situated in a crowded red brick fortress surrounded by graying two-family homes, enrolls 570 young adolescents, of whom a growing 70 percent are Negro. Of these 400 Negro children some 160 are coming in from outside the district—electing to attend the Holmes under Boston's open enrollment policy because it seems (either to them or their parents) preferable to the Campbell or the Lewis Junior High Schools which they would normally attend. The Campbell is 98 percent, and the Lewis 100 percent, Negro. Holmes' administrators point out that the school's own district is not imbalanced (it comprises a lower-middle-class area in Dorchester), and that, as recently as 1961, it was less than one-fourth Negro. Imbalance, they imply, was created ironically through the free choice of Negro parents, and not through any deliberate or even accidental pattern of segregation. Charles B. Kenney, the principal, describes the newcomers as children of parents who are "well off economically," children of small Negro businessmen, lawyers, and civil servants who have come to this school for "prestige reasons" (or, perhaps, because it represented the best alternative to an otherwise totally segregated situation). Although Kenney reports spending considerable time on the problems of "kids in trouble with the law," in parental conferences, meetings with police authorities and truancy cases, the school continues to remain attractive because it has what many Negroes consider the only assurance of educational success —enough white children to constitute reasonable assurance of administration interest and good instruction. Holmes has, moreover, a battery of remedial and enrichment services: after-school music and art and science programs, special developmental reading classes for all children which, the administrators claim, produce two years' advancement in one year (no substantiating figures were available), and a variety of other special classes conducted during and outside school hours. There are jazz concerts and glee club performances, after-school movies, intramural athletics (before school opens), and a variety of clubs for children willing to spend an extra hour or two in school. ("A pet snake and some small animals conveniently died in the science lab," said one of the school's official reports on the afternoon activities, "allowing a number of interesting dissection sessions for students.") Nevertheless, a majority of the students are reading below grade level for their particular ages.

The basic program at Holmes is divided into two tracks, one "academic" (about one third of the students), the other "general." Students are placed in the tracks on the basis of assessments made by administrators on the potential of the pupils. In practice, even the best of Holmes' pupils, no matter what their track, go to the district high schools and then, if they are lucky, to business institutes and junior colleges. The academic track includes some French, while the general program has a heavier emphasis on shop and general business courses. But the core of each track, with some

94

variations in degree of sophistication, is similar to the other. The Oliver Wendell Holmes Junior High School offers all students history and civics, mathematics and English, geography and science, all taught according to traditional styles.

In a seventh grade history class taught by Archie Walsh, one of Holmes' two assistant principals, the students are answering questions about the American Constitution. Walsh, a small, tough, competent professional—an educational Mickey Rooney —asks questions with a machine gun staccato and gets responses, right, wrong, and ambiguous, with equal speed.

Q. Did we win the Revolution, Foote?

A. Yes.

Q. Of course we did . . . So then we had to establish a plan of government that was called what?

A. The Constitution.

Q. I'll hit you in the head. (Hands are up.)

A. The Articles of Confederation.

Q. What were they? (Pages flip in the textbook.)

A. Our first plan of government.

Q. Why did we drop it? (Confusion.) What was the matter with the Articles of Confederation?

A. They weren't strong enough (More hands are up, more shuffling of feet.)

Q. What happened at the meeting to alter or change the Articles?

A. They decided to drop them and make a new plan.

Q. There were two main weaknesses in the Articles. What were they?

A. They could make laws but couldn't enforce them.

Q. It's the same as in the cafeteria. If there weren't any teachers there, if Mr. Walsh wasn't there with his whistle, there'd be bedlam. Would there be a change in rules? No. There'd be a change in government because the rules weren't being enforced. We need rules, not laissez faire . . . Now for tonight I want you to think about what is a compromise. I want you to make up your own compromise . . . Now open your books to the section about the three branches of government. What are they?

A. (All students in unison) Executive, legislative, and judicial.

Q. Say it again.

A. Executive, legislative, and judicial.
Q. Again.
A. Executive, legislative, and judicial.
Q. Congress makes the laws for whom?
A. Makes the laws of the United States . . .
Q. For all or part?
A. For all of the United States.

The class is alive; the questions and answers snap. Hands wave. The students respond quickly, in a rhythm that they have learned well since the beginning of the year, and which now has a life of its own, apart from the substance of the material. Most of the answers come in phrases, or in short sentences—brief declarative statements in response to factual questions, with rarely a dependent clause or a connecting word. This is drill, and to perform one must know the answers before the questions start. The questions lead to a string of data, like a quiz carried on from day to day, with no logical end, and with no inductive thought. History, in most American classrooms, is still one damn thing after another.

To administrators like Kenney and Walsh, the major problems at Holmes stem from the attitudes of the kids and from the limitations of the building itself. "Ever since the second school boycott (organized on a city-wide basis by the NAACP in 1964) there's been a scofflaw attitude," Kenney said. "Some of the parents supported that boycott through a fear of reprisal; many of them know that there is just as much concern for the education of Negro children as of whites, and that the same books and courses of study are offered. After the boycott there was a kind of demoralization; the kids came back with chips on their shoulders and started quoting all the rules and regulations about what we could or couldn't do. We're not different from other schools. I've heard this elsewhere." Kenney is trying to "keep the area clear" of older boys (there have been several pregnancies among Holmes girls) and to deal with an endless string of minor offenses: truancy, runaways, and even occasional cases of car theft and robbery. ("There's real respect for teachers here," said a member of the Holmes staff. "When there's trouble outside the school—in the yard or on the street—the teachers usually handle it because they can do it better than the police. The cops get sass from the kids.")

Kenney is proud that the school's many special offerings have drawn interest, even enthusiasm, from the students. He is pleased by his programs of compensatory education (especially in reading), with his intramural basketball (conducted before school each morning), and with attendance at the afternoon music, art, and science classes. During the winter of 1966 about 80 kids took part in these activities each week, among them a number from other schools. At the same time he and Walsh have been nearly overwhelmed by the limitations of the building in which they must operate, a structure planned more than sixty years ago for another age and other conditions. Since there is only one small gymnasium which must be used alternately by boys and girls, all civics classes (for example) are composed entirely of students of one sex. While the boys are in gym, the girls are in civics, and vice versa. Since the cafeteria is hopelessly overcrowded, the brief twenty-minute lunch periods are further subdivided by staggering the moment when the children at each table may line up at the serving counter for dessert. (Walsh blows his whistle and calls: "All right, table five may get their jello.") Library space and resources are inadequate; there is no language laboratory, only the most rudimentary science equipment, and not a spare corner where either teachers or pupils can enjoy privacy. Such limitations make academic flexibility—even if desired—almost impossible. A student who gets out of line or asks irreverent questions becomes not only a minor offender but a threat to the whole social order. Every move, every course, every maneuver through halls, doorways, lunchroom, must be planned and organized: the triumphs come from operational and managerial success, the failures from deviation and inadvertence. In a small storage closet Walsh maintains a large schedule board covered with small cards, each of them representing one class. To him, understandably, the ultimate challenge is to make certain that everything is planned and accounted for; the ultimate reward is that everything goes as predicted.

The physical limitations at Holmes—as at other schools—are matched by limitations of personnel and program, and by managerial attitudes committed to lesson plans, careful organization, and academic predictability. Holmes, for example, has one guidance counselor for its 570 students (some junior high schools have one for 1,000 students); it has only one science teacher, offers only one foreign language—French, and provides only the most restricted opportunities in shop and science. (Some junior high schools offer two languages, as well as work in printing, drafting, electrical work, and sheet metal. Holmes' vocational courses are limited to "clothing," "foods," and woodwork.) But most administrators do not see these limitations as serious problems; indeed they seem to regard them as Spartan virtues inculcating discipline, frugality, and self-restraint. The schools, they point out, are orderly, efficient, and clean; classes are run without confusion or disturbance. "The Ivy universities are supposed to be the saviors, with their new ideas, and all," said one teacher. "But I've seen supposedly bright teachers from Harvard get taken apart in these classes and then saved by some little guy from Boston State who knew how to handle the kids. What good are all those ideas if you can't control the class?" As far as the hierarchy on Beacon Street is concerned, the junior high schools are doing splendidly: each year, in the official Boston school report, they are described as "maintaining their high standards of performance" and "high level of efficiency." The school reports are silent about overcrowding, carry no photographs of the dismal buildings, no statistics describing the varying levels of academic success and failure. The pressing questions regarding the function of these schools are left untouched: should they track children into "academic" and undefined "general" programs? Should they offer technical and academic preparation that would fit students for vocational training and retraining after they complete high school? Should they continue as three-year schools at all, or would it be better to plan for a 4-4-4 system (four years of elementary school; fours years of intermediate school; and four years of high school)? The assumption of the School Department is that everyone knows what a junior high school (or any other school) is and should be, and that these things have always been known, They are the assumptions of people so committed to the *status quo* that they hardly know anything else exists. And yet, each year the junior high schools of Boston graduate kids whose reading abilities are about two years below the national norm.

* * *

"Our philosophy of elementary school education," says an official circular from the office of the deputy superintendent, "is the orderly and harmonious development of the physical, social, civic, intellectual, aesthetic, and moral powers of the child. Through instruction, controlled experiences, precept, and example, the child must be educated for a complete and productive life in conformity with the laws of God and of our country." According to this philosophy:

> The school develops and expands social relationships in a rapidly changing world. It recognizes that dramatic changes and manifold problems are inherent in our urban society. It stresses the principle that all rights and privileges entail obligations and responsibilities. It encourages high standards of group behavior so that the child may become a good citizen, appreciative of his dignity as a person, and of his moral accountability to himself, to his fellow men, to his country, and to his God. It provides those experiences by which duly constituted authority is understood, respected, and obeyed; it also assumes responsibility for corrective action when necessary.
>
> The school helps to prepare the child for economic relationships. It instills an understanding of the world in which he lives, a respect for sound American enterprise, and an appreciation of those who serve in the world of work. It inspires every child to continue his education in order to become a productive, self-supporting individual, adequately prepared to compete effectively and to contribute his share to our American democracy, and to further the progress of mankind.

The statement, significantly, says nothing about teaching children to question and challenge, to be curious, or to enjoy. It assumes that they must be brought into "conformity" with the going order, and that this order (despite the fact that one fourth of the kids are underprivileged) is satisfactory and healthy. It assumes that the children are, or should be, willing to accept the values of the system, that, indeed, the whole function of the schools is to bring children into harmony with the society as the operators of the schools conceive it.

The most articulate spokesman for the elementary schools in Boston is Marguerite Sullivan, who, until her retirement as deputy superintendent in 1966, directed those schools and who, for many people in the system, personified the stern-but-kind schoolmistress looking out for the best interests of her children. "The schools," she said, "are less patterned and structured than they used to be. But the kids haven't changed a bit." Miss Sullivan, a striking, white-haired woman of seventy, has probably adjusted to change more easily and sympathetically than the male bureaucrats who surround her—and than the schools themselves—and she can thus say, with some grace and ease, that "we're interested in process; we're not concerned with packaged knowledge." Rita Sullivan is a wholehearted defender of the system, but, as she reviews four decades in the School Department, she is probably more aware of the problems and difficulties than anyone in the system. "The schools are going to be 50 percent Negro quicker than you think," she said shortly before her retirement. "In the past 18 months the Negro enrollment went up by 2,800 and the whites declined by 1,800. How can anyone expect our kids to be on a par with the suburbs considering all the advantages those kids have? We've got to open up new jobs and housing, and we've got to try new approaches. We have to prepare them to move out into the world." Miss Sullivan is a great enthusiast of compensatory education for deprived children—called Counterpoise in Boston—which, she feels, has improved motivation and attendance and has increased specific reading and arithmetical skills. (No figures available.) Counterpoise was designed to "stress a strong language arts and arithmetic program, raise aspirational levels, stress personal appearance and good grooming, and bring about positive changes in behavior and attitude toward school." Teachers who staff it are urged to maintain contact with parents, to insist on "the highest standards of behavior," and to emphasize work in arithmetic and language arts. Like compensatory programs in other cities, Counterpoise has become a major weapon in the system's defense against charges of mistreating or disregarding children of racial minorities.

Miss Sullivan's prime concerns—which she shares with most of her colleagues—are directed to "building values" and attracting competent teachers. "The community," she feels, "is expecting us to take on more and more. We have to build values." Although she said that children have always been the same, her descriptions suggest that, in fact, they are not, that the motivated have left, and that the deprived, the children of relief and welfare and broken homes remain, and that they are no longer the same. And in this she expresses the feelings of most of the classroom teachers and principals of every district in Boston.

* * *

"I'd like to say that the neighborhood appreciates this school," said a teacher at the John F. Kennedy School, Boston's newest (1964). "But you should see the broken windows. And the parents probably stand around and watch the kids do it." The Kennedy School, located near a low-income housing development in Jamaica Plain, enrolls about 600 children of whom about 40 percent are Negroes, many of them from the projects nearby, and they represent all the symptoms of family decay and deprivation. "Our biggest problem," said one of the teachers, "is the parents. Many children lack a father image. The better youngsters, academically and emotionally, have both a mother and a father."

"Of course some of us get discouraged," said Thomas F. Kennedy, one of the assistant principals. "There are days when you feel that way." To Kennedy, the new building doesn't make much difference. "The key to success is a good teacher. With a good teacher you could hold class on the Common in a blizzard." Nevertheless, in the tone of the school, in the bright displays, the lighting and the movable furniture, the Kennedy School generates an atmosphere of cheer and confidence, an uninstitutional quality that the old dark buildings do not share. There is, indeed, no reason why good education cannot take place in a factory or a warehouse; and yet no parent or child or teacher is unaffected by the surroundings. In a decent building teachers are not required to succeed in spite of the building; they can succeed with it.

Sally Donahue's fifth grade class of thirty pupils could be taking place almost anywhere. Some of the children badly need haircuts and a few need new shoes or blouses, but in this setting those deficiencies are somehow less apparent. There are pictures and maps on the walls, and there is a sparkling energy in the interaction between teacher and students. The illustrations indicate that currently *we are doing Alaska*:

Q. Why would they go by dog sled?
A. Because there's a lot of snow.
Q. What's the land like along the coast, Michael?
A. Mountains.

Q. What do they do on the coast?
A. Hunt?
Q. What do they do on any coast?
A. Fish.
Q. What kind of houses do they live in?
A. In dirt huts . . .
Q. What is a tundra?
A. A treeless plain.
Q. Good . . . Now where is the far north near? I should see more hands than this . . . Andrea?
A. The North Pole.

She continues her questions—about animals and minerals, "the islands where we find the seals," and about what the children invariably call "the ice-free hahbahs," gently reinforcing correct answers and disregarding errors. Mrs. Donahue, without doubt, is building some sort of confidence, but like the teacher down the hall who is asking "Where does the story take place?", like Archie Walsh at Holmes, asking them to repeat "executive, legislative, judicial," like the analysis of "To a Waterfowl," the class, inevitably, leads only to another fact lifted from a book, and then to another, and another. These are not the social facts of experience but the staples of an official liturgy. They may lead to the understanding that people who live near the sea engage in fishing or that a tundra is a treeless plain, but when do they generate a sense that the world is full of facts and ideas waiting to be discovered, and that most of them are not in textbooks? Where are the teachers and classes devoted to inductive learning, producing the sense that *any* subject (and taught at any level) is a human construct, a way that the human imagination organizes experience to make order out of chaos? Where is the school that tolerates confusion as the price of a self-generating, self-reliant intelligence? Where are the classes engaged in examining not the official mechanics of the American government (let alone the Soviet government) but how a tenant can get action from the housing inspectors or how a neighborhood can organize to clean up a playground? Who acknowledges that the world does not operate according to textbook descriptions? Where is the ironic voice, saying what many of the kids already feel—that the prescribed program does not in fact explain the society in which most of them live? What teacher communicates to his class the sense that he really understands this world, that he is not some curious creature from a different world, a world committed to classroom charades about people in costumes and wigs? It may, after all, be true, as Thomas Kennedy said, that the building does not make much difference. Clearly the Kennedy School building, unlike Holmes, does not impede relevant education. But it does not create it either.

* * *

For some time, the all-Negro W.L.P. Boardman School was the best-known elementary institution in Boston. The school, located at the edge of an incomplete Roxbury urban renewal project, stands like a ragged tooth against the demolition rubble to the North. In 1964 the parents of its 200 pupils asked that it, too, be demolished on the ground that it was old and inadequate, but Boston cannot afford to tear down old schools, and the building remained. Thereupon the parents organized a protest and began to bus their children to the Faneuil School at the edge of Beacon Hill, halfway across town, leaving Boardman with an enrollment of 60 in a building intended for more than three times that number. Many classes had no more than ten children, and a few had eight. In April 1965, when Martin Luther King, Jr., came to Boston, he tried to visit the Boardman School but was refused admission by the authorities. (His picture, along with those of other well-known Negroes, now hangs inside the building.) King thereupon started his famous march through Boston, protesting *de facto* school segregation, on the steps of the Boardman School.

In the fall of 1965 the school was taken over by the Office of Program Development, the research and development staff headed by thte imported Evans Clinchy, and it is now tthe keystone of Boston's most ambitious experiment with culturally deprived children. The administrators call the project focused at the Boardman School a "subsystem," a phrase that probably comes from the jargon of the federal programs supporting it and therefore can't be blamed on Boston. The subsystem, simply, is an effort to create complete model schools, to break the cycle of educational futility, rather than to rely on separate, isolated programs. Boardman, supported by part of a $3.6 million federal grant, represents an attempt to pull out all the stops.

When the subsystem took over the Boardman—choosing it because it was, thanks to the boycott, one of the few uncrowded schools in Roxbury—there was a complete turnover in staff. Clinchy asked for volunteers willing to work an eleven-month year (the extra month for planning and study) and a week described as "seven hours longer than normal." At the Boardman, someone explained, "nobody leaves before three o'clock." (The standard day in other elementary schools—until 1966, when state law prescribed a somewhat longer school day—was 8:30 A.M. to 2:15 P.M.) The volunteers were carefully screened for background and experience: demoralized veterans from the boycott era were replaced by younger men and women with as large a diversity of background as one can find in Boston. Anne O'Neill, the principal, is a product of Boston State—Boston Normal when she went there—but there are also alumni of Boston University, the Massachusetts College of Art, and teachers now enrolled as graduate students at Harvard, Tufts, and Northeastern. There are, moreover, Ivy League representatives in the corps of experts and volunteers—students and academic planners from Harvard, Radcliffe, and Simmons—employees of Educational Services, Inc., the private organization of curriculum developers in Watertown, Massachusetts, and, infiltrating the building, a variety of educational theorists and planners of every conceivable sort: game learning experts, teachers of eurythmics (a dance or series of movements set to music), from the New England Conservatory of Music, instructors in vocal and instrumental music from Boston University, and purveyors of packaged exhibits of birds, Indians, and other displays from the Boston Children's Museum.

With access to the outside specialists, and to Clinchy and his staff, the regular teachers hold periodic planning and review sessions ("we try to discuss problems and offer solutions"), trying to examine just what succeeds and what does not. During their breaks—this is one of the few schools where members of the staff enjoy such a luxury—they discuss process learning and new materials, structured curricula and the ungraded system. They are intelligently self-conscious of what they are about, and, if they are still far from being even partially successful, they have at least begun to ask the right questions.

Boardman is being developed as an essentially ungraded school with small classes—no more than 25 per room—and with the freedom to try whatever materials, techniques, and ideas seem most appropriate. Thus the idea of a "subsystem" describes not only the effort to build a model school, it also means, in the negative sense, freedom from the administrative routines and restrictions that Boston normally imposes on its schools. Attempts are being made to form an active group of parents—some of the same people who pulled their children out two years ago, to enlist community volunteers as classroom aides, and to identify special problems as soon as they occur. "Actually," said Miss O'Neill, looking over her shoulder at the rubble beyond the building, "the kids here are less deprived than they are in some of the other Roxbury schools. You see only a few without socks, and there aren't more than one or two who come to school without breakfast. More than half of the children have both parents living at home. I've met some of the fathers. . . . We're trying to keep close contact with the families. The trouble in most schools is that you don't know the families of the ordinary kids unless there's a problem." Miss O'Neill feels that the community's early suspicions, set against a long history of mistrust and conflict, are beginning to fade. She also feels that "there's a real spirit in this school—among the staff, and the parents, too." Part of the evidence for that spirit is the fact that the Boardman, which had a residue of 60 despondent pupils in 1965, now has a waiting list for most of its classes. (Some parents, nonetheless, are still busing their children out of the Boardman district.)

The walls and stairways of the Boardman School are cluttered with conscious attempts at cheer and uplift; there are scores of drawings made by the children, inscriptions enjoining everyone to "Let Us Be Proud," photos of prominent Negroes: Leontyne Price, King, Massachusetts Attorney General Edward Brooke, U.S. Circuit Court Justice William H. Hastie. Everywhere there are reminders to be clean, to obey, to strive. "We try not to be grouchy," said Miss O'Neill. "We want to control, but not for control's sake. When I came to the school tardiness was pretty high; I was very cross. Now we're down to four or five tardy a day."

In Walter Sweeney's second grade classroom—Sweeney is the only male second grade teacher in Boston—the children are giving short talks that Sweeney is trying to transcribe with a tape recorder (which isn't working properly), telling about what they like to do, and then responding to the questions Sweeney poses about the Negroes whose pictures are taped to the wall under an inscription stating "By Our Own Efforts . . ." Sweeney's hope is to develop a confidence and competence in spoken English— which many of his pupils lack. Some have rarely spoken complete English sentences—have indeed rarely heard a complete sentence. Their homes are places where dialogue is often limited to two-word injunctions and one-word replies— Get that, go away, pick that up, close the door, shut up, yes, no, don't—and where some children learn early to tune out all but the loudest noises—where life is lived above the cries of children, the chatter of television commercials, and the riot of urban decibels rising from the street below. "You know," Sweeney said, "on the first day of class, I asked them to form a line in front of the desk. I thought they were pulling my leg, but they couldn't do it. I had to place them."

"Now let's use our very best English and our best brain," says Sweeney, pushing a button on the recorder. "Now, Jacqueline, what did you do on your holiday?" From outside comes the noise of jack-hammers and heavy construction equipment.

"We went to the zoo."

"And what did you see at the zoo, Jacqueline?"

"A man had a snake around his neck."

"What else did you do?"

"We had turkey."

"Did you help cook the turkey?"

"Uh-huh."

"Did you wash the dishes?"

"We both wash the dishes."

"Now let's talk a minute about these gentlemen here." He holds up the microphone of the tape recorder. "Which one do you want to tell us about?"

"That one."

"This is Mr. Whitney Young. He's the president of the Urban League. Now what do you suppose urban means?" Hands go up. Jacqueline stands awkwardly before Sweeney's microphone. At last a rotund boy stands and announces that urban means houses.

"Yes," Sweeney says. "We can be proud of Mr. Whitney. He builds houses for our city. He helps make our city clean and beautiful. . . . Well, thank you, Jacqueline, now let's see if we can play this back." He rewinds the machine and starts to play the conversation, but one can barely hear Sweeney's bright voice, and Jacqueline almost not at all. When the children can understand her they giggle at her uncomfortable replies.

"Now who wants to tell us about this gentleman," Sweeney continues. "His name is John Hope Franklin. Who knows what an educator is?" The rotund boy survives the melee of waving hands and incorrect answers.

"He's something like a teacher," he replies.

"That's correct," Sweeney rejoins, writing on the board as he says: "Mr. Franklin is a famous teacher." Then he returns to the pictures. "Now this man, his name is Thurgood Marshall. He's a judge. He's very honest . . . Now all these men are great workers for what?"

"For the United States," a girl replies.

"That's right, Lorraine. They are great what?"

"Great people?"

"Great men?"

"They are great Americans," Sweeney assists. "They are great Americans."

"Now it's your turn, John. Come up here to the microphone and tell us what you want to talk about."

John speaks about a visit to his grandmother, then another child describes the visit of his sister, explaining, when asked, that Carl Rowan, then the director of the U.S. Information Agency, "works for President Johnson. He's a detective."

"Now why did we tell those stories," Sweeney asks, giving up on the recorder. "How many people feel embarrassed standing up here to talk?"

"They itch," a child volunteers. (Giggles.)

"What do you mean—they itch?"

"They wiggle."

"What are we supposed to do when we talk?" Sweeney asks.

"Stand."

"Don't wiggle."

"Talk loud."

"Yes, and we must use our very best English and our best brain."

Like every slum school, the Boardman inherits a network of

social and private problems, some of them created by the conditions of life in the ghetto, some of them simply the normal accumulation of family trauma, of personal injustice, of the bitterness that personal tension and friction generate even—and especially —among children. In a combined fourth and fifth grade mathematics section the teacher has discovered, for example, that Juan, a Puerto Rican boy, has mastered long division while his twin brother, Manuel, is unable to produce a correct answer. Their father encourages and reinforces Juan, while Manuel, who never says a word, has been firmly established at the bottom of the family pecking order. In every test conceivable, the boys seem to be identically competent, but Juan can do the work while Manuel cannot. Thus the teacher devotes himself to repairing the damage, but, after six months, he has done no more than to extract a few words from the boy, the only success to date. "All right, now divide 750 by 25 . . . how do you check it?"

"Multiply . . ."

"Very well . . . Now try this: 450 by 30 . . ." The boy stands impassively at the board, scratching down the numbers. The teacher moves to another child where numbers and symbols are rapidly fading under the smear of erasures and moist palm smudges. The physical process of carrying out the arithmetical operation conspires to frustrate success; it is hard for anyone to understand the computation under the chalk smears that surround it. "Okay," says the teacher, "now do you have anything left?"

"No," says the child.

"Now how do you write no?" The child places a zero after the number. "Oh God love you," the teacher exclaims.

For teachers not concerned with producing success, the task of instructing deprived children is comparatively simple: follow the manual, and blame failure on low motivation, poor background, broken homes, or anything else that makes sense—but always point to difficulties outside the classroom. The problems become serious when the situation or the teacher demands success, when you, as a teacher, have committed yourself to be flexible, and when you are told that you are not bound by the curriculum ("There must be no independent seat work activities," says one of the elementary curriculum guides). Then, even though you may conclude that Manuel's trouble stems from his father, or that Jacqueline, who comes from Florida, has never heard proper spoken English (which is not to say that they do speak it in Boston), or that the kids haven't learned how to form a line, have perhaps never been to a department store, have never ridden an elevator, then—despite all these handicaps—you must begin to figure out what you, in the classroom, can do. You must determine what the problem is: is it cultural deprivation or family deprivation, is it lack of food, or limitations of language experience, or is it limited intelligence? Can the child hear satisfactorily, or has he just learned not to listen, responding only when someone shouts? He seems to enjoy drawing and, fortunately, you, in this special school, have a full-time art teacher, but you have also been told that you cannot neglect reading and arithmetic, that sooner or later you must try to convert drawing into language, into written words and sentences.

The teachers at the Boardman School have committed themselves to an attempt to deal with all these problems, to communication with parents and with community groups, many of which exist not because of confidence in the schools, but because of mistrust. In their first year of trial they treated their experiments gingerly; their strength was not in combining two or three grades for mathematics or English, not in the discovery approaches of the new mathematics, not in Walter Sweeney's tape recorder, but in their self-consciousness, and in the systemic opportunities to exercise it. What they have demonstrated is that freedom from restrictions—sometimes simply the time to reflect and discuss—can produce a level of morale that a collection of overburdened classroom clerks held together by the official rule book cannot possibly achieve. The people at Boardman are a long sight from being revolutionaries; for some of them, nongraded classes may be all right for the brighter children, but not for slow ones ("Clinchy is hot on ungraded classes," one said); for others, discovery learning, by which children are encouraged to work out their own induced conclusions, is, at best, a noble cliché, and, for most, good behavior and spelling-book maxims about ambition and hard work are still essentials of classroom success. (Martin Luther King, at the Boardman School, is not a rebel. He is a hard worker.) But even though their model school has barely completed its first year, even though they lack test scores and other objective measures, they have already demonstrated what, tragically, must be demonstrated again and again, and that is that when teachers are given a little time, are treated like professionals, and are given the freedom to function, they will respond.

"The *big* experiment," said Evans Clinchy, looking over the papers on his desk, "is whether an office like this can work." Clinchy, who has become Boston's presiding potentate of innovation and development, was hired by Ohrenberger in 1964, after having been associated with both Educational Services, Inc., and with Educational Facilities Laboratory. He has rarely been in the classroom at all. His offices are now in the old Academy of the Sacred Heart, recently acquired by the Boston system from an order of nuns, and converted to an elementary school and offices, still complete with crosses and statues of the Virgin testifying to its former ownership. Clinchy's problem is to break barriers inside and outside the school system, to overcome the hierarchical conservatism of one and the hostility against the system on the part of the other. Working with $3.6 million in federal Title I funds (money allocated by the Elementary and Secondary Education Act to systems with large proportions of deprived children), Clinchy is responsible for coordinating the educational research and development activities of the area universities with the programs of the Boston schools, for the system's joint programs with Action for Boston Community Development, the city's antipoverty agency, for the planning of the new 5,000-student campus high school, which, eventually, is to become part of the "subsystem," for the general supervision and planning of new buildings, the general planning of new proposals for federal assistance under the Elementary and Secondary Education Act, and, finally, "for the improvement of the school system as a whole, indeed, for making the Boston schools a model for urban education all across the country." In brief, Clinchy, at least on paper, has the responsibility for making Boston a modern relevant school system.

The Office of Program Development, Clinchy feels, is a reflection of the fact that for years the Boston schools were, oddly enough, underadministered. "Ohrenberger was simply understaffed." In 1963, after Francis Keppel had become U.S. Commissioner of Education, President Nathan M. Pusey of Harvard, then also acting as dean of the Harvard Graduate School of Education, called Ohrenberger to suggest formal ties between the University and the Boston schools, much as Harvard already had ties, especially for teacher training, with suburban Newton and Lexington. Concurrently Ohrenberger had received a grant from Educational Facilities Laboratories to plan the new campus high school. Clinchy, who came from EFL to advise on the high school planning, thereupon assumed not only the job of coordinating the new university connections, but of directing other educational development as well. He became the agent of modernity in Boston. Clinchy has no civil service rank, no foothold on the hierarchical ladder but, he said, "I've been struck by how openly I've been accepted by the School Committee."

In fact, he has not been fully accepted either by the School Committee or the administration. His appointments are more often challenged than any others; his programs create more confusion and silent hostility, his educational attitudes produce more resistance than those of any other administrator. "The federal government thinks this is a great frankfurt deal," said William J. Cunningham, the associate superintendent to whom Clinchy is theoretically responsible. "The government doesn't give us enough time—there's too much rush to plan professionally sound programs. There's this terrific emphasis on preschool programs but there's no hard evidence that they're worthwhile. All this growth and development is too fast for us. I think we're losing sight of the average kids."

Clinchy, nevertheless, is pushing as hard as he can, not only for specific innovations and the growth of the subsystem, but also to influence the whole set of educational attitudes that have held the city in a straitjacket for a generation. "We have to find out more about the urban kind of kid," he said. "We want to experiment with the process-oriented approaches of Jerome Bruner [essentially inductive discovery learning] and with the techniques of Sylvia Ashton Warner [in which the children compose stories that are used as the basis for instruction in reading]; we're taking over the Head Start program and trying to provide more cultural enrichment. Naturally we hope eventually to affect the rest of the system." Concurrently Clinchy and his staff, some of them part-timers from Harvard, some recruited from ESI or from the Boston teaching force, are trying to enlist the support of the Roxbury community. "There's a tremendous amount of hostility against the school system," he said, indicating what everyone already knew—that the community, given the attitudes of the School Committee and the long history of recrimination, would meet his efforts with suspicion. After his first meeting with Roxbury parents, Mrs. Ellen Jackson, the leader of the Exodus parents, who are busing their children out of the ghetto, challenged Clinchy's program as too vague. (The Exodus group has no formal connection with the Boardman parents group, which is still busing its children from that school to the Faneuil School near Beacon Hill.) "We'd been told that the Boardman School would be run by Harvard, that this school would be separate from the system," Mrs. Jackson said. "But it's not. Harvard does not have the last say. We want the school to be open until nine at night, but they aren't willing to do that. I don't think they really want to collaborate with the community. They just want to tell us what to do." Clinchy's problem, essentially, is that while he is not fully accepted by the School Department, he is too much part of it to be trusted by the parents. He cannot afford to be a real revolutionary, cannot even pretend that he is one. And while he tries to talk cooperation, the School Committee continues to alienate the community with gratuitous insults and rigid policies indicating that, while it may be fashionable to take federal money for innovation, there has been no change of heart. The hope that Clinchy will eventually influence the system, that he will make himself so indispensable—for money, if nothing else—is still a long way from realization. Clinchy himself is one of the few school administrators, in Boston or anywhere else, who regard federal money as an opportunity not merely to add new programs or to do more of the same, but to reform entire systems. In public appearances he has been critical of those systems that use Title I funds to support programs that are essentially additive, and that are not designed to reshape existing practices. "In the light of many existing school programs," he told a group in Washington, "all children are deprived." For a school administrator, *that* is a revolutionary thought, even outside the Hub.

But in Boston, the big experiment is, indeed, to see whether an office like Clinchy's can succeed. In its brief existence to date, it has produced in the Boardman School one promising, though hardly startling, innovation, a lot of mimeographed plans, and a considerable amount of federal money. But it has not begun—despite

Clinchy—to talk real radicalism or even, given what is already known about urban education, real innovation. It has captured neither the enthusiasm of the community—nor, probably, of the children—nor have its mild proposals really affected the system. It is, despite its ambitious staff, too little, too meek, too pious, too detached, and too conservative. Innovation, Boston style.

* * *

Over the years, the Boston schools, like those of many other cities, have compiled an uninterrupted record of negative progress. The city is not dealing exclusively with Negro children, although, as Marguerite Sullivan said, they may soon be in the majority. But it is dealing with children, black and white, who are very much the victims of the same kinds of educational deprivation and of the same kind of academic mythology. Most of them are from working-class homes, some of them from the unemployed working class. As a consequence they depend on formal educational institutions in a fashion that upper-middle-class children do not. (A recent federal study indicated that the quality of education seems to affect children of lower-income families much more significantly than those whose families have the cultural resources to offset deficiencies in the school program.) As they go through school they fall farther and farther behind the national average. The typical child in Boston has a reading achievement of 5.6 in the sixth grade (the national norm is 6.0) while the typical child in predominantly Negro districts reads at 5.1, almost a full year behind. By twelfth grade those discrepancies double. Boston's Negro parents complain that the ghetto schools are underequipped, that they offer little effective vocational training, that they have a high rate of teacher turnover—some children have as many as four teachers in a year—and that the buildings are dirty and dangerous. Mrs. Jackson, for example, feels that in the schools to which Exodus is busing children, there are smaller classes and that "even though they may have the same books there are enough to go around. They have things like phonographs, and teachers with better attitudes."

Many of these differences are immeasurable. Boston's schools lack so many things, are often so crowded, that discrimination is sometimes hard to establish. The Negro schools do not appear to be substantially worse than those that are predominantly white, although they are often far more crowded. The Negro districts, with their growing numbers of Negro children, are the chief victims of the city's failure to build new schools. But there is one subtle, yet significant, element of discrimination: in their adherence to old attitudes about behavior and good conduct, and in their tendency to link criticism with *bad* conduct, many teachers and administrators identify middle-class, lace-curtain characteristics with effective education. Within the schools one hears constant remarks about "our good relations between the races," about how "our Negro children are just wonderful, they're so well behaved." There is a patronizing atmosphere about *all* children in the Boston schools, a sense in which they are regarded as incomplete human beings who must be ministered to, who must be manipulated and managed, and whose success as students depends on a positive response to that manipulation. The application in the classroom of the standards of the Irish home, the rigidity of the mixture of Yankee and parochial school techniques, the commitment to an old morality—all at the expense of independence—impose themselves far more severely on Negroes than on whites who have been to the manner born, and who are less committed to good education in the first place. To a self-conscious urban Negro of the nineteen sixties, a general patronizing attitude, even when it involves no discrimination between races—and often, in subtle ways, it does—strikes at the very respect and dignity he attempts to achieve. Boston tends to treat all school children like second-class citizens; for the Negro, trying to achieve first-class citizenship—and having rarely found it—that treatment appears especially reprehensible.

The city's school administrators assert that their problems reflect the problems of urban schools everywhere, that one can't expect children from the inner city to perform on a par with middle-class suburban kids. And yet, so far, they have done little to mitigate the differences. They are introducing Negro history, and texts with pictures of Negroes; they are adding afternoon and summer classes for deprived children, and expanding compensatory classes (essentially just more emphasis on language fundamentals) to more schools. But they have shunned genuine radicalism or even reform, preferring to retreat to defensiveness, to their traditional conservatism (in the old days kids had the right attitudes), to tired platitudes about motivation and success. A few years ago James Baldwin made some significant proposals to a group of New York teachers:

> I would try to teach Negro children [he said]—I would try to make them know—that those streets, those houses, those dangers, those agonies by which they are surrounded, are criminal. I would try to make each child know that these things are the results of a criminal conspiracy to destroy him. I would teach him that if he intends to be a man he must at once decide that he is stronger than this conspiracy and that he must never make his peace with it. And that one of the weapons for refusing to make his peace with it and for destroying it depends on what he decides he is worth. I would teach him that there are currently very few standards in this country which are worth a man's respect. That it is up to him to change those standards for the sake of the life and the health of the country.
>
> I would suggest to him that the popular culture—as represented, for example, on television and in comic books and in movies—is based on fantasies that have nothing to do with reality. I would teach him that the press he reads is not as free as it says it is—and that he can do something about that, too . . . I would suggest to him that he is living, at the moment, in an enormous province. America is not the world and if America is to become a nation, she must find a way—and the child must help her find a way—to use the tremendous energy which this child represents. If this country does not find a way to use that energy, it will be destroyed by that energy.

The teachers of Boston would find such an attitude frightening. They do not know how to deal with it. Their loyalties and training are all with the established order, committed to rote learning and discipline; and they assume that it is their prime function to introduce and adjust children to that order. This is their declared function, their practicing creed, their reason for existence. This is what schools do.

Socially and pedagogically, the schools of Boston are immigrant schools. In their concern with character and middle-class values, and in attributing academic failure to the inability of poor children to be like everyone else, they are operating according to standards and assumptions characteristic of the melting pot schools of half a century ago. They are trying to Americanize—according to the ideals of another age—children whose problems are already all too American and therefore not susceptible to the treatment that folklore associates with the functions of the common school of sixty years ago. It is, of course, perfectly true that Boston, like other cities, is losing its middle class, and that the children now in school do not have the social and cultural background of those who have fled. But it may also be true that the attempt to shape them in the old image will prove futile, and that the techniques of Horatio Alger and Ellis Island can never be the keys to success. The urban kids are not greenhorns just off the boat. They are not starting on the American ladder to success. Many of them—black and white—are children for whom, in some sense, America—not Italy or Greece or Ireland—has failed, children of families that cannot accumulate enough of what Daniel Moynihan calls cultural capital and who are trapped in a cycle of economic and social futility. The fact that others have succeeded, and that educational officialdom constantly holds that success up to them, makes their failures all the more frustrating and damaging. And yet, constantly the schools—in Boston, in Chicago, in Topeka— are trying to shove the kids back on the ladder, insisting that if they only had the right attitude, only wanted to succeed, they would. The schools never suggest that much of the problem lies with the social order, rather than the kids or their parents; they are rarely on the side of reform or change and never acknowledge what many of the children have already learned: that the civics books formalities of the classroom have little to do with the life they know in the city—that you can't get to see the mayor when you wish, that civil rights are very much affected by who you are and how much you can pay, and that the idea of initiative is all too often a club used on those who haven't made it.

Boston's educational program is pathetically irrelevant. It is true that there are good teachers, but they succeed despite the program, and then only with students who are already motivated. As a program it makes sense only for those who see little value in powerful education in the first place, or who have accepted a subservient, limited image of themselves and their possibilities. It pays lip service to the idea of independent thought, to an emphasis on process, but it practices preaching and the accumulation of facts about irrelevant details. For the deprived it stresses "language arts," which, God knows, they need, but it ignores social self-defense in favor of "the highest standards of behavior"—that is, the passive acceptance of the *status quo*. It stresses "free enterprise" but ignores the vicious damage that it inflicts; it talks about the democratic society but fails to acknowledge the corruption that exists in profusion in every community, and in the slums with a vengeance; it demands haircuts and neckties but ignores the vulgarity and ugliness of the buildings in which they must be worn; it upholds the value of the individual but denies him the right to go to the john without a pass; it eulogizes the historical right of protest but patronizes those who now attempt to exercise it. At every turn it belies itself, confesses to being fraudulent, hypocritical, and stupid.

Boston—and other cities—like to talk innovation. Innovation has become fashionable and profitable. The federal government will pay for almost anything billed as new or experimental. In the past two years more than two billion dollars have gone to programs associated with education for "disadvantaged youth." Around the urban school systems are magnificent necklaces of special programs, head starts, pilot schools, enrichment classes; but the body of education and the results produced remain almost unchanged. In Boston, which has enough trial programs and experiments to fill a book, the life of the average child in the average classroom is virtually unaffected. The teachers, the curriculum, the school committee are the same. The books are the same. The attitudes are the same. All of them insist that this is the best of all possible worlds. But it is not.

AROUND these sad and crowded schools with their debris and broken windows, their ancient halls and peeling paint, swirls a continuing controversy that has, if anything, become more strident since the 1965 election. The emphatic voice of the Boston voter, Gartland's defeat, and the Hicks victory failed to discourage the critics, the prophets, and the saviors. After the initial shock and bitterness, they seemed to produce new efforts, new schemes, new plans to save the schools of the city and, if possible, to provide an example for other communities confronting similar problems and similar intransigence (if not in degree, then certainly in kind). In the storefronts of Roxbury, the parlors of Newton, and the offices of the Harvard Graduate School of Education, earnest and often competent people wondered how to turn the tide, how to help the children, how to pressure, ameliorate, convince, or seduce the School Committee into new policies and attitudes. New counselling and tutoring programs were organized by neighborhood associations and the area colleges, and there were new groups of volunteers who offered their services as teachers' aides. A group calling itself the Council for the Public Schools put 220 women to work as aides in the schools, and an organization of college students and professors, operating under the aegis of Harvard, Brandeis, Tufts, and other universities, secured federal funds through Northeastern University to operate a college and vocational counselling center on Blue Hill Avenue. There were plans for metropolitan school arrangements, for independent community schools, for federal investigations and state action, and—perennially—for a constitutional change abolishing the elected School Committee altogether, and for replacing it with one appointed by, and responsible to, the mayor. People said that *this* time, something will change, that the pressure of the state, which had already started to withhold funds, or the subtle influence of Harvard or some other force will produce a change of heart. For two or three months Mrs. Hicks disappeared from the front pages of the newspapers, disappointed, some said, because she was no longer in the chairman's seat at the School Committee, sentenced to oblivion, said others, because the editors finally realized that they helped create her, and had now banished her from the front page. (In fact neither was true. If she had decided to run for mayor she would not have had a chance until late 1966, and then only if Collins were elected Senator. Otherwise not until the regular city election in November 1967.)

When the post-election hiatus ended, and when the State Board of Education began to show signs of a stiffening attitude regarding racial imbalance, the battle was resumed. Although Mrs. Hicks rarely appeared on the local front pages in the early months of 1966 (she was, however, featured in *Look* and the *Alantic*) the struggle continued to be identified with her. Inevitably segregation—despite the universality of inadequate education in Boston —overshadowed academic conservatism, hierarchical stultification, and the perpetual political funk emanating from the School Committee. By and large, it was the racial issue that continued to draw attention to the schools, and Mrs. Hicks who symbolized segregation. Negroes, more than anyone else, made education a real issue in the city.

* * *

A cold morning early in February. The chartered yellow Exodus bus rumbles slowly north on Blue Hill Avenue, past second-hand shoeshops and clothing stores, the Roxbury office of the Neighborhood Youth Corps, and Muhammad's Black Muslim Temple of Islam standing behind a blue sidewalk awning around the corner on Intervale. Then, with difficulty, it turns right into Lawrence, backing up to maneuver between a parked Dodge and the gray snowdrift on the other side, then down Lawrence. There are eighteen Negro children on the bus, ranging in age from eight to perhaps thirteen, and of all sizes and shapes. They boarded the bus at 378 Blue Hill, the headquarters of Exodus, where a man named Frank Silva acts as the dispatcher who organizes the routes and assigns the 400 Exodus children to the proper vehicles—buses, cars, and taxis. (There had been 300 in September, when Exodus began.) Until this year, many of these children attended the crowded Greenwood, Gibson, and Endicott schools in Roxbury. But early in the fall their parents decided they had had enough. If the School Committee, which allowed children to move to other schools under an open enrollment policy, would not provide the transportation, they would do it themselves, and Exodus was launched.

It is 8:05 A.M. In the back of the bus sits a boy with a transistor radio, listening to the artificial excitement in the voice of a morning wake-up announcer, and next to him another boy who is holding up a glistening chocolate lollypop. "If my father drove this bus, the motor'd fall out," says a strident voice from the front.

"There goes a Sting Ray," somebody shouts.

At the corner of Columbia Road and Washington Street, the bus waits as a girl slowly approaches on the walk.

"Here comes that fat Minnie," says the boy with the radio, shouting, "Hey, Minnie, you're a balloon."

"That's Minnie," someone rejoins. "She waddle."

The bus proceeds, with Minnie aboard, turning left into Hewins Street and then, cautiously, between a parked car and a bakery truck, into Erie. This time the driver must stop the bus and back up twice in order successfully to round the corner. A large heavyset boy is waving his hands at an expressionless girl in the seat behind him. She hits him with her purse. Then the boy kicks a smaller boy sitting across the aisle. The smaller boy hits back, keeps hitting the bully who, of course, is now justified in kicking harder. The driver stops the bus to break up the fight. "You do that anymore and you won't ride this bus again. Now you sit up here by yourself." The noise on the bus momentarily diminishes, although the children near the front haven't bothered even to turn around. The radio is still going. The driver returns to his seat and the bus proceeds, passing a few small stores and two-family houses standing behind piles of dirty snow and, along the curb, the garbage cans waiting for the day's collection. On a blank wall adjacent to one of the stores is a large sign urging "Buy

Israel Bonds." As the bus turns into Talbot it picks up two more passengers, then it rattles on, over the bumps and ruts, to Codman Square, one of the centers of Dorchester, where the Girls Latin School is located. The noise has mounted again. Someone from the back calls a boy in the front: "Hey, your sister have that party?"

"Uh-uh, she get sick."

"Bam, bam, bam," a wiry little boy calls out, banging a tin lunch box. "Bam, bam, bam."

Do the children like these new schools? They have been going there now for six months, riding this bus twice each day.

"Yeah, it's nice," says the girl who hit the bully with her purse. She is still expressionless, and speaks without much feeling.

Why is it nice?

She shrugs her shoulders. "The teachers are nice." Another child explains that the books are nicer. "They aren't ripped."

"Hey, what you saying to that man?" calls a voice. "Bam, bam, bam."

With a change of light the bus now crosses Codman Square, crosses Dorchester Avenue, and moves into an attractive neighborhood of single family homes separated by lawns and driveways, stopping finally at the Ellen H. Richards School on Beaumont Street, where some of the children get off. It is now almost 8:40. The bus proceeds, stopping soon again at the Minot School, and then again at the Kenny School, where it discharges the last of its passengers.

The sheer problem of negotiating the turns, of winding through the narrow streets between the parked cars, the garbage cans, and the snowdrifts, gives a special ironic meaning to the idea of the neighborhood. It is not simply hard to escape the Roxbury schools, but to leave Roxbury itself. The physical geography of the city isolates sections, impedes transportation, and helps choke the social and educational traffic that great urban areas are supposed to foster. Robert Coles, a psychiatrist who has studied the impact of desegregation on children, and who has often traveled on the Boardman bus, has described the educational impact of the different neighborhoods through which the children travel. To him the act of busing itself is a positive educational experience. And yet it is clear that the bus, running from one section to another, is the most segregated of institutions, the most confining of conveyances.

Perhaps, in this age, it is, more than anything, a symbol, a plea, a gesture of desperation. It testifies to the failure of community and to the failures of education. To the fearful the bus is a totem of all that is socially destructive, a hateful sign of civil rights aggrandizement destroying the delicate social arrangements of home and neighborhood and convenience. It is a final reminder that the city is not the village and that the neighborhood—often impersonal and private, and usually ill defined—is meaningless, a magnificent myth shattered by transiency and public disregard. But in the city the bus is also an impractical cumbersome machine, a big yellow blockade with flashing red lights adding another burden to an already overloaded transportation grid.

Every school day in 1965–66 the Exodus buses made their journeys from Roxbury to schools deep in white Dorchester and Hyde Park, running a stern and continuing (and expensive) rebuke to the Boston School Committee. And every week Mrs. Ellen Jackson and Mrs. Betty Johnson and the other Exodus mothers raised between $1,200 and $1,400 to keep the buses rolling. Beginning in September in an empty storefront that they shared with the Northern Student Movement, they posted signs and issued handbills proclaiming:

> 8367 Seats Available
> in 63 Schools Outside
> Of Roxbury
>
> Why Send Your Children to
> Overcrowded Low Quality Schools?
>
> Come With Your Children Here
> Monday at 7:30 A.M.

and:

> Parents Rally
> Sunday September 12
>
> Protest Overcrowding
> Plan for More Busing Monday

and:

> Benefit Cabaret and Dance
> Given by Parents and Friends
> of Operation Exodus

Featuring the Calypsonians
and Elma Lewis Dancers
February 11

Later they moved to their own office, contributed by a Roxbury landlord on Blue Hill, and subsequently redecorated by the Exodus fathers. From there they now operate the busing program, direct their various benefits, and operate tutorials for school-age children. Help came simultaneously from other sources: the parish priest of St. Hugh's Roman Catholic Church on Blue Hill Avenue made the church basement available for meetings; Wellesley College students and suburban housewives conducted fund drives, a civil rights organization at M.I.T. raised $1,200, an *ad hoc* organization in Cambridge, Belmont, and Newton sent another $1,200, and, for a time, another donor supported the expense of a bus "in memory of Pope John XXIII"; there were charity dances and mothers' marches, benefit dinners, bake sales, and house-to-house collections. Eartha Kitt and Odetta gave benefit concerts. Concurrently the Exodus fathers started a youth program in athletics and other activities, the mothers began to solicit information on classroom discrimination to send the federal government, and initiated a research program to determine the effect of busing on the children.

"We were tired of the paddling, of teachers pushing children against the walls, of temporary teachers and poor buildings," Mrs. Johnson said. "We're quite convinced that children in these crowded Roxbury schools weren't learning as much as those in other schools. The parents in the different schools had been talking for some time about the quality of education. When the School Committee refused to bus children out of these crowded schools, when they wouldn't accept the recommendations of their own administration, which proposed busing, we began to work through the parents' organizations to start Exodus."

Exodus demonstrated that the Negro community could be organized, and that action could be directed not only toward protest, but also to positive self-help. Ellen Jackson, the other Exodus co-chairman, and one of the most dynamic people in Roxbury, expects that the campaign is only the start of a mounting drive to improve education in Boston. As she sits behind her desk at the Blue Hill office, answering phone calls and solving an endless series of minor crises ("You must have asked for two tickets . . . Well, then send them back" . . . "Which bus was that? Was it the same driver? . . . What did the child do?") she declares that Exodus will continue, and that other techniques will be used to improve the schools. "Yes, we're tired, physically and mentally," she says. "But it's something we have to do. We can't afford to let the children sit there and vegetate. We're going to bring more pressure on the schools, through the state, the federal government, and the local neighborhood. An awful lot of people have become involved. They're running surveys and collecting money, taking children to youth concerts, and tutoring. People just come in to ask if there's something they can do."

Where Exodus or its successors will go after the first year is still open to question, although it was clear by late summer that the program would continue in the fall of 1966, that it would transport more children—it had applications for 1,000 places on the buses—and that it might even get federal support, perhaps as much as $250,000, from the U.S. Office of Education. The Exodus parents are convinced that their children have benefited educationally, and there is no evidence to indicate that they are wrong. "Most of us," said one of the mothers, "feel that our children have made vast improvements. There were smaller classes, and it seems as if the kids had a better chance. They could talk with the teacher more often and explain their problems." Another mother explained that for the first time their children had access to musical instruments, that each pupil had a dictionary and that, most important, each was treated with more respect and more attention. Much of the future, of course, will depend on the attitude of the School Committee itself, and on the effects of the financial pressure that the state, through the Racial Imbalance Law, is bringing to bear. But it is certain that Exodus, probably the most significant protest against educational discrimination of the year, was only the beginning. Even while it was going on—and partly because of it—other organizations were being formed and other plans formulated. Simultaneously the School Committee, collectively and as individuals, made it clear that very little has changed in Boston since the 1965 election, that they remain as adamant as ever about desegregation and redistricting, that there will be no busing, that despite the pressure of the state, the answer is still "never." Exodus, therefore, is only part of what will increasingly be one of the most significant educational battles in America. Perhaps *the* most significant.

* * *

So far much of the battle has been characterized by isolated skirmishes, by the exchange of gratuitous insults and gestures, to symbolic acts having little bearing either on educational substance or on school integration. Its major issue has been the development of a plan of desegregation that will be acceptable to the State Board of Education under the Massachusetts Racial Imbalance Law, and even that became, at least for a time, a kind of game—a series of Geneva conferences where, alternately, X and Y find each other's proposals unacceptable. In April 1966, under the aegis of the State Board, a staff member at the Joint Center for Urban Studies of Harvard and M.I.T. submitted a plan involving some redistricting. Under it, for example, the almost totally white Cleveland Junior High School in Dorchester would henceforth be composed of 480 whites and 360 Negroes, while the Holmes Junior High (165 whites, 400 Negroes) would be composed of 370 whites and 200 Negroes. Only a minority of Boston's school districts were to be affected, and even those changes involved serious policy problems. (For example, what if Negroes under open enrollment, renewed the imbalance by shifting their children?)

But well before the plan—not even called a plan, but only a list of suggestions—was formally submitted to the School Committee for discussion, one of its members leaked it to the papers while Edmund H. Barry, the principal of the Cleveland School, showed it to parents. An uproar ensued. Within hours Eisenstadt received more than a hundred phone calls from the indignant in Dorchester, a hurried press conference was called, and denials issued. "Proposals of the state task force have no force or effect unless they are approved by vote of the School Committee in public meeting," Eisenstadt declared, "I urge the organizers of protest meetings to cease their activities until this tempest in a teapot subsides. Such a meeting can only generate more confusion." Eisenstadt went on to call the proposal radical and to chastize Barry for leaking it. Barry also called the proposal radical and replied that "I am amazed that an elected public official would withhold from parents information that vitally affects their children's lives." Thereupon Eisenstadt received more calls and letters of invective from neighborhood patriots who told him that if he supports busing or redistricting "there will be another member elected to the School Committee next time."

Almost simultaneously Mrs. Hicks climbed back into the papers. Appearing with McDonough and O'Connor at a meeting of the Field's Corner Neighborhood Association of Dorchester, she declared that there will be no redistricting, that the state suggestions were "made by a computer which didn't take into consideration the emotions of the citizens." It was almost like being on the political hustings again. "You need not fear," she added, "that this plan will ever go into effect, because we have the votes against it on the Committee." A few days later, after Associate Superintendent William Tobin, who had been negotiating with the state, called the proposal unsound ("It would do more harm than good," said he), the plan was officially killed by a 3–2 vote (Hicks, O'Connor, and Lee), with McDonough and Eisenstadt voting that at least it be considered. To replace it, the committee sent back to the state a list of expedients that relied on a vague proposal for an $108 million building program, a reiteration of open enrollment, the expansion of compensatory education and cooperation with the Boston Housing Authority in making more new housing available to nonwhite families. As expected—and almost immediately—the State Board rejected it, declaring that "this is not the time to stress what purportedly cannot be achieved but rather is a period when vigorous educational leadership will demonstrate how the values of integrated education can be accomplished." The Board, adopting the recommendations of a special task force headed by Deputy State Education Commissioner Thomas J. Curtin—who may be the most disliked man at 15 Beacon—declared that open enrollment has been a failure as a method for reducing imbalance, "except insofar as programs have been organized, financed, and carried out by private groups." It also urged Boston to develop plans whereby the number of Negro students in all-Negro schools would be reduced by 2,000 by October 1966 and that would eliminate imbalance in at least four of the 46 imbalanced schools. "Redrawing school district boundaries and the providing of transportation assistance," said the board, "should be considered as assets to be utilized in developing a workable plan rather than obstacles to its realization."

"Exactly what I feared would happen did happen," Eisenstadt said. "Our plan was good as far as it went but it didn't go far enough." He predicted that the whole issue would go to the courts where, he said, the constitutionality of the imbalance law would be upheld, and he proposed a summit meeting with the state board to discuss the matter. At that point, instead of sending the educational statesmen of the School Department back to try for another plan, the committee defiantly voted to resubmit the proposal that had already been rejected by the state, and to stick with it. Eisenstadt, now more than ever the voice of reason, pleaded that "there is a law we must obey," and then tried to strike directly at the Hicks myth. "One conveys to the electorate an image of courage," he said, "when he stands up as a solitary individual against the giant of the state. In this instance, at best, this is a false image, simply because it is a false and hollow courage. Hollow, because by defying the state we, as committee members, have nothing of material value to lose. It is the taxpayers who will lose." Despite this bit of eloquent reason, the majority of the committee —Mrs. Hicks, McDonough, and O'Connor (Lee was off on a different tack)—remained unmoved. O'Connor added his own little sentiment by declaring that there is no evidence "that integrated education is educationally desirable. The problem," he added, "is not the teachers but the failures of the parents." Then he joined his colleagues in sending back the old proposal, an act that was tantamount to a declaration of war on the state board and the imbalance law it was supposed to administer.

At this point the heretofore farcical negotiations became more serious. A few weeks after the School Committee resubmitted its plan, the state froze another installment of funds designated for the Boston schools, bringing the total withheld to approximately $16 million. (Massachusetts Commissioner of Education Owen Kiernan estimated that the figure would reach $32 million before the end of 1966.) O'Connor reasoned that since the state formula for school aid allocated half this money for construction, and since the committee couldn't seem to get any new schools built anyway, it didn't make that much difference. It was clear, however— O'Connor's cheerful thought to the contrary notwithstanding—

that if the system did not get the funds, it would confront a financial crisis of the first magnitude. For the first time in history, Boston (and other communities) were eligible—under a new legislative formula—for a sizable chunk of Massachusetts money. These funds, derived from a sales tax adopted earlier in the year, would support almost one third of the Boston school budget, and that budget, as well as the city tax rate, was based on the expectation that the money would be available. Now all that was in serious jeopardy. Toward the end of the summer, therefore, the School Committee filed suit to recover the money on the ground that the law under which it was withheld was unconstitutional. Eisenstadt, although he voted with the committee to file the suit, was confident that the law would be upheld; Louise Hicks was certain it was invalid. Now the judges of the state courts—and perhaps eventually the federal courts—would settle the matter. In the meantime the money was in escrow. And so, in a sense, were the schools and the children.

Despite their serious and potentially tragic overtones, however, the negotiations with the state were not earning anyone on the committee many political points. Although the papers gave the matter front-page attention—the *Globe* called the committee's decision to reject the state plan a "mockery of the law" and attacked the three majority members for their lack of concern "over the economic harm their action will precipitate through loss . . . of State aid"—and although other critics of the committee attacked it for its continuing indifference to both Negroes and hard cash, there was little drama in an exchange of memos, statements, and letters. There were no protests or boycotts, no personal confrontations. After the flurry over the initial leak and the reaction of the Cleveland parents, good gutsy emotionalism was lacking. No one seemed to care. The school year was ending, vacations were approaching, and the weather was growing hot. The vitriolic season was almost over.

Then, just as everything settled down to a dull routine, ruffled only by the abstract possibility of a permanent loss in state aid, Mrs. Hicks, mistress of the innocent insult and symbol of all that is reprehensible in the professional world of civil rights, demurely appears on the platform at the graduation exercises of the overwhelmingly Negro Patrick T. Campbell Junior High School in

Roxbury. She represents the School Committee and is ready to say a few words to the 140 graduates, of whom 137 are Negroes. As the glee club finishes a rendition of "The Battle Hymn of the Republic" and students prepare to line up for their diplomas, the militant Roxbury minister and civil rights leader Virgil Wood enters the room and begins to approach the platform. "This is a very serious matter, Mr. Principal," he shouts. "Would any synagogue invite Hitler?" As he mounts the stairs to the platform, people in the audience begin to chant "Go home, Mrs. Hicks." Since someone had expected that there might be trouble—had in fact persuaded Mrs. Hicks not to pass out the diplomas, a function often performed by the visiting School Committee representative—there were eight plainclothes policemen in the crowd, and they began to close in.

"Is Mrs. Hicks interested in our children?" says Wood, now speaking into the microphone.

"No," shouts the audience.

"Does she belong here today?"

"No."

"What do you want to say to Mrs. Hicks?"

"Go home." The principal, Francis E. Harrington, speaks to Wood, who returns to the microphone.

"The principal of this school, who doesn't live in this community, just asked me to leave. Who should he ask to leave?"

"Mrs. Hicks." Then the cops move in, carry Wood from the stage and into a hallway behind the auditorium. "Leave him alone, he's a minister," someone screams. People in the audience begin to rise and push and shout. A garbage can sails over the crowd, barely missing two women. Wood is still shouting as the crowd begins to pursue the police into the halls. In the confusion, Wood, now in his shirtsleeves—somehow he has slipped out of his coat—returns to the platform.

"I see Mrs. Hicks is still here," he shouts. "Do you have a message for her?"

"Go home, Mrs. Hicks."

"Mrs. Hicks is a trespasser here today. There's a new day in this community. God's message has come down for freedom." He turns directly to Mrs. Hicks, still seated at the rear of the platform in her white suit, white hat, and white gloves. Behind her, on the wall, hang some drawings done by the children. "Go on home," says Wood to the Great Mother. "You don't belong here. I ask you to leave. You really don't care about our children." Mrs. Hicks stares at him, expressionless.

"Get her out, get her out," people shout from the crowd.

"I'll go," says Wood to the principal, "provided Mrs. Hicks goes too." There is a brief conference between Mrs. Hicks and the school officials, and then, escorted by policemen, she leaves the auditorium and goes to the principal's office where, according to the newspapers, she sits for more than an hour. As promised, Wood leaves also, and the children are taken into two classrooms, the boys in one, the girls in the other, where they receive their diplomas. In the meantime, more police have arrived in the school, and others wait a block away, just in case there is a real riot. But this part of the affair is over. (Wood is later arrested and charged with disturbing a public assembly.)

Another symbolic act. Four days after the Campbell commencement, some of the civil rights leaders hold a "Freedom Graduation" at St. Hugh's Church. (They had requested use of a school building. Eisenstadt indicated that that was asking a little too much.) The speaker at St. Hugh's is the six-foot-ten-inch Bill Russell, star and coach of the Boston Celtics basketball team, now billed by a Boston sportswriter as "the tallest man ever to give a commencement address." Only a handful of the Campbell graduates are there—one commencement a season is probably enough for anybody—but there are 700 other people in the building.

"The Negro in Boston is being systematically eliminated from the mainstream of the economy," says Russell, reading his speech. "There's a fire here in Roxbury that the School Committee refuses to acknowledge, and the fire that consumes Roxbury will also consume Boston. Because of a lack of real communication, a polluted atmosphere hangs over our cities, an atmosphere of hate, distrust, ignorance, a complete lack of knowledge of each other. I do not say that we have to love each other, but we must try to understand and respect each other." Russell's boss, according to Boston sports writer Bud Collins, is not particularly pleased. "I know he's right," says Red Auerbach, the former coach and now general manager of the Celtics. "But I don't want people using him, or him going around making a lot of speeches. His job is coaching, and he's got to learn that a coach or a manager can't take sides politically."

"Why am I here?" says Russell in reply, and the reply becomes more eloquent than the prepared speech. "Because I was a Negro man before I was a coach, and because I'll be a Negro man after I'm through as a coach. I've always said what I thought, and people are bright enough to know it's still me, and that I'm not representing the Boston Celtics here. The people of Roxbury are important to me, and so are the people of all of Boston. The schools are bad everywhere in the city—this is every citizen's fight, not just Roxbury's . . . I spend most of my life in Roxbury because of my business [a restaurant called Slade's]. And this woman—we don't mention her name any more—came in and insulted the people of Roxbury. This woman ran on a segregationist ticket, and then she comes to the graduation and flaunts herself. That was an insult. And she was looking for an incident. And she provoked it, the thing with Reverend Wood . . . I don't think I would have done what he did, because it's just what she wanted. It put her back on page one again. Actually I think the reaction to her that day was mild. I think that any other racial group would have harmed her if she had insulted them as she did the people of Roxbury . . . There is potential for violence in Boston this summer. That's why I'm with these people tonight who are trying to tell Boston what is happening to its children because of this School Committee. There must be change."

* * *

There must be change. There must be change in school districts and academic practice. There must be change in facilities and attitude. There must be change everywhere in this historic and now decaying system. But almost all the changes discussed are fragmentary, or symbolic, or, in some instances, self-defeating. It is hard to reform a system in which most of the staff, most of the electorate, and much of tradition are against you. It is hard to revolutionize an ancient city, hard even to know what you want ideally to achieve.

In a Roxbury church a young white novelist named Jonathan Kozol is meeting with a group of Negroes and whites to plan, or at least discuss, something called The Community School. The proposed school represents one of three separate attempts (two others were abandoned) to secede from the Boston system and, with private money, establish new independent institutions. According to Kozol's original prospectus:

> The educational program will be very finely tuned to the needs of the children in the school—it will truly be a pupil-centered school; an atmosphere of freedom will pervade the school; it will exemplify the ideals of our democratic system; and the life of the school and the life of the community will be seen as inseparable, the one serving and depending upon the other—it will truly be a public school.

Kozol, a former Rhodes Scholar from Harvard, was for a time a temporary fourth grade teacher in the Boston system, but was fired —in another minor *cause célèbre*—for offenses that included his reading in class of Langston Hughes' poem "Ballad of a Landlord." But whether it was this or simply the fact that Kozol is, in every respect, the very antithesis of the Boston teacher no one in Boston wants to say. Now, as he stands before the small group (perhaps forty people, more than half of them white) he looks like a jacket drawing for a Kafka novel—thin, white faced, with large steel-rimmed glasses, faded blue denim shirt, rolled up tightly at the sleeves, and a dark tie—trying, as he said later, to keep the dream of the school in the realm of reality. His intention is to be democratic, to avoid running away with the meeting, but he is also uncertain. After all, this is supposed to involve Negroes, but at this meeting the whites from the South End are more visible and vocal than the Negroes from Roxbury.

So far the school has neither a building, teachers, students, nor books. It is merely a hope, and even the hope is not yet very distinct. "We thought at first we would have one library for the whole school," Kozol says, "but now we have been told that a library in each classroom is better if we intend to go through seriously with individualized reading." He explains that the school will probably be ungraded, and that teachers could specialize in certain areas, one in science and mathematics, another in "social science," another in "humanities and literature." What it suggests is a progressive preparatory school for the motivated, liberal middle class, not a community effort in the slums.

An exciting and valuable learning environment [the prospectus says] can only be created where there is freedom—freedom from fear, freedom from shame, freedom from meaningless and unnecessary constraint, freedom to love, freedom to choose, freedom to disagree . . . . It should not be necessary to point out that these freedoms will pertain to children, teachers and parents equally. In an atmosphere of freedom, children, teachers and parents can participate in that community of learning that is the ideal of education. . . .

The children will not come from any one neighborhood or religious or racial or ethnic group. It will be a truly integrated school drawing from the population of the city at large. The same principle applies to teachers, parents and scholars. Furthermore, all will have their role in the school. Although it will be the teachers' responsibility to design and carry out the major share of the educational program, parents and professional educators will work closely with the teachers whenever and wherever possible. Parents will take their place side by side with the teachers and will help to work with the children in a variety of ways. Some, it is hoped, will eventually develop into extremely effective teachers themselves.

Education in the community school will not begin at eight and stop at two thirty. To the community of people who comprise the school, education will never cease. The school will be a center for learning and for the exchange of ideas at all times. . . . Ideally, parents, teachers, and educators will learn as much as children.

The meeting continues. It is explained that the school, born at least in part of the desperation that followed the 1965 election—and now, obviously, endowed with a different significance—will have a pupil-teacher ratio of fifteen to one, that it will enroll about 100 children between the ages of five and eleven, and that it will use team teaching, independent study, and programmed learning "where they are seen to be appropriate." Various members of the planning committee report on recent gifts, among them two of $1,000 each and one of $500. There is a vote on whether to establish a permanent office (affirmative) and another on the name for the school. Shall it be called the Nova Children's School? Or the New Children's School, or some other name? (Under his breath, someone waggishly suggests calling it De Facto Prep.) There is discussion of a possible site, and of the need for a director; does anybody know a good candidate who would be interested? (It is already May, and the school is supposed to open in September.) There is more discussion of educational planning and philosophy, allusions to self-fulfilling prophecies and viable alternatives, and more representations of democratic equality and the community of scholars.

But the school does open, despite its uncertain beginnings. By September 1966 the group has rented a house in Roxbury, it has enrolled 79 children, about three-fourths of them Negroes, and it has four experienced teachers and a Negro woman principal who has taught for eighteen years in the public schools of Chicago. Support comes from tuition and from contributions solicited by the Friends of the New School for Children. In its first year—as the School seeks accreditation—there are four grades and a kindergarten, there are frequent class trips through the city (the children write stories about what they see, not what the system feels they are supposed to see), and there is a warm, relaxed atmosphere which, according to those who have visited it, contrasts sharply with the rigid formality of the Boston system. "You know," said a Boston reporter, "when I walked in the door, the children didn't rise in unison to say 'good morning.' But one little kid ran up and kissed me."

* * *

There must be change. In Newton, Brookline, Lexington, Wellesley, Braintree, and Arlington, the school committees have voted to join a collaborative program to bus about 240 children from the slums so they can attend suburban schools during the 1966–67 academic year. Brookline will take 100 children in grades 3–12; Lexington will take 25 at the junior high school level, Newton 60 at the intermediate level, Wellesley 30 in grade 10, Braintree 20, and Arlington 15. Together they have formed an organization called Metropolitan Council for Educational Opportunity— Metco—the first regional effort in public education in the Boston area, and one of the first anywhere in America. Reluctantly, the Boston School Committee agreed to participate in Metco, provided it would not cost the city anything (Boston almost immediately used Metco as an argument indicating compliance with the imbalance law).

Metco, largely the inspiration of an M.I.T. faculty member named Leon Trilling (he is also a member of the Brookline School Committee), represents the first formal effort of the suburbs to come to the aid of the deprived children of the city, the first duly ratified enterprise to discharge some of the responsibilities that the flight from the central city imposed. Financed by a $239,000 grant from the U.S. Office of Education and by a smaller grant from the Carnegie Corporation (for staff and office), Metco will cost neither Boston nor the suburbs a cent; at the same time, with an average outlay of over $1,000 per child for tuition and busing, it matches in cost the most expensive public education in America. (At Metco's rate, the Boston budget would double.)

The leadership of Metco reflects the growing alliance between the suburbs and the slums. Other elements of the city are not represented. Its directors include Trilling; Paul Parks, the education chairman of the Boston NAACP; Laya Wiesner (wife of former presidential science advisor Jerome Wiesner), an officer in the Massachusetts League of Women Voters; Charles Brown, Superintendent of Schools in Newton; Betty Johnson of Exodus; David Sargent, the chairman of the Wellesley School Committee; and several other residents of Lexington, Wellesley, and Newton. Metco, they feel, will "develop and promote quality integrated education, provide opportunities for integrated learning experiences, and develop modes of cooperation in education between urban and suburban school systems in the Greater Boston area. Metco's initial program is designed to be a first step towards solving the problems of *de facto* segregation in Boston schools." They add, however, that they will not relieve Boston of the responsibility for solving its own segregation problem. "Nearly 24,000 Negro children will still be attending Boston schools. . . . Metco is expected to focus steadily increasing attention on the Boston schools."

With a program similar to one proposed in Hartford by a team from the Harvard School of Education, Metco's leaders are persuaded that their busing operation will help not only the Negro children, but also the suburban whites "who have been cut off from contact with children of other races, to the detriment of the education and total development of members of both groups." Embarrassingly, a number of white Boston parents also asked to send children to the suburbs, but they were politely refused. "We know it's discrimination in reverse," said a Metco leader privately, "but we've got to do it this way." (No one has questioned the federal government about the legality of this application of government funds.) The children, who volunteered for Metco (or whose parents volunteered them), were selected by the receiving school systems for their academic potential on the basis of scholastic records supplied by the Boston School Department. Each school day during the academic year they are to be bused from centers in Roxbury and Dorchester to the suburban communities and then returned at the close of the school day. In each suburb the child is to have a "second home," a family which will handle emergencies, help provide "local social contacts," and attempt to develop a personal friendship with the child's own parents—a combination, finally, of Exodus and Friendly Town.

In promoting the early stages of Metco, the founders made every effort to reassure suburban parents that the Metco kids would not deprive the locals of anything, that they would not become a horde of city savages descending on the salubrious greenbelts, and that they would not consume educational services intended for the resident children. Often they succeeded, sometimes producing a genuine pride in the effort. Suburban parents pointed out that only through metropolitan collaboration could the cities hope to solve their educational problems; many volunteered to provide "second homes" and to staff some of the nonprofessional jobs that Metco involved, all of them feeling that they were engaged in a pioneering effort that could have major consequences in other cities. But there were also instances when the reaction was violent and negative, when suburbanites felt that the very *raison d'être* of the suburbs (middle-class exclusiveness?) was being jeopardized.

In Wellesley, perhaps the most conservative corner of the affluent periphery, a group styling itself "Concerned Citizens"— among them several of the local members of the John Birch Society —conducted a poll, ostensibly to determine whether the citizenry favored the idea of "busing non residents" into the town schools. (Actually it meant thirty Negroes at Wellesley High.) Advocates of Metco, which had already been approved by the School Committee, called for a boycott of the referendum which, as expected, resulted in an overwhelming endorsement of the anti-Metco position. A total of 1,249 votes were cast; of these about 80 percent were negative. With the results in hand (the advocates of Metco, of course, denied their significance) the Concerned Citizens went to the School Committee where, on a warm spring evening, they got their chance to be heard.

In a packed elementary school cafeteria, the School Committee chairman, David Sargent, himself a director of Metco, explains that the committee is interested in new information, in legitimate expressions of opinion directed to the committee, not in a community debate. The committee is there, he declares, to learn, not to make statements or to educate the public. Then the statements begin.

Lawrence Gosnell, one of the anti-Metco leaders, explains how the poll was conducted, then reports that in a conversation with an official of the U.S. Office of Education, he was told "that if we want to withdraw from the program we may do so. We ask for a full legal review."

"We want to make sure," says another speaker, "that we keep the federal government from gaining more control of our school system."

"Let's not wrap Wellesley up in some social experiment. Somebody down at the FBI building in Washington told us that once the Communists gain control of education they have a tremendous grip."

"What about the students," says a Metco advocate, "what do the students think?" In the back of the room a young man rises and declares that although he is speaking as an individual, he, as president of the Wellesley High School Student Council, wants to report that in a poll of the thirty council members, twenty-eight were in favor of Metco.

"I'm more concerned with what adults think than what children think," someone says. "We're the ones who go to the polls."

"Mr. Chairman," calls a man from the rear. "We have been told that this is not a racial matter. But of course it is a racial matter. For years I lived in the heart of Roxbury. I have nothing against Negroes, but I know that once these people come into the community they will impair the schools. This program is just for the colored."

"There's no legal justification for the School Committee to get into Metco. You're supposed to tend to Wellesley education."

"A reappraisal would be in the Wellesley tradition."

"The federal government is supporting this program," says a Metco advocate, "not the taxpayers of Wellesley." (Groans. The chairman bangs his gavel. This is for information, not a demonstration, he says.)

Another Metco defender asserts that the program will enable "the city and suburbs to pool their strengths. It's still premature to expect the formation of a greater Boston school district, but at least we can do this much. Perhaps ultimately we will be able to develop other programs, perhaps an exchange of teachers or joint curriculum planning." Then the School Committee reaffirms its earlier decision. "The outside world," says one of the members, "is not going to be segregated. There is a great need in Boston and there will be advantages in this for Wellesley students. Personally, I don't think we're doing anything heroic for Roxbury."

"This is an experiment," declares another member. "It may not work, but we've got to try it."

Outside the building, the leaders of the Metco opposition hold another meeting, collecting names of sympathetic persons, and declaring that this is only the start of their campaign.

"Are you planning a recall campaign?" a reporter asks. "What do you expect to do?"

"We're just collecting names and discussing strategy," someone replies. "We have plans but we're not ready to disclose them. . . ."

"Why don't you let the kids decide?" a man shouts from the gathering. "What do they think?"

"The kids decide? They're not old enough. What do they know?"

"We bought the schools, didn't we?" another man says. "We paid for them." Names are taken, and one of the leaders announces the number of a post office box where the committee can be reached. Then the crowd disperses to the ranchwagons, Impalas, and Imperials standing in the parking lot, and melts into the well-groomed streets.

* * *

There must be change. In the living room of her apartment in Mattapan, a Jewish neighborhood just inside the city limits, Mrs. Ralph Nathanson, the president of the Boston Home and School Association, declares that the schools' biggest problem is "apathy." What is lacking, she says, "is enough interested people. In the small town participation is a way of life. Here there's a lack of communication. It's hard to find out what's going on."

The Home and School Association has often been called a company union; it has an office at 15 Beacon Street and an administrator paid by the School Department. By its constitution it is forbidden to attack the schools. "But," Mrs. Nathanson says, "the administration has never suggested that there are things that the association should and should not do." She concedes that she has been closer than most association presidents to the people at 15 Beacon Street, but that, she feels, is because of a personal interest and a long concern with the system. (In some circles she is considered an apologist for Mrs. Hicks. Mrs. Nathanson denies that.)

Since Boston has no parents' organization other than the Home and School Association—no nationally affiliated PTA—the association with its 52,000 nominal members represents the most important formal channel of contact between parents and teachers. All teachers belong to the organization and, by charter, the presidency alternates between a teacher and a parent. (Mrs. Nathanson's successor was to be Archie Walsh, the assistant principal at the Holmes Junior High School.) The separate district organizations in this federation raise funds for school equipment, and they serve as a vehicle for school communication with parents (and, occasionally, for parent communication with the schools). But the association has never been committed to reform—and, neither, with some exceptions, have the local groups. They are too much wedded to the rest of the system. At no time in the battle for racial balance or in the extended controversy about educational quality has the association become militant, or even critical. It does not criticize the administration, the School Committee, or the conduct of the schools. Mrs. Nathanson is pleased that "the schools don't jump with both feet into every new experiment," and not at all sure that the schools should make greater efforts to bring in administrators from the outside. "I'm fed up to here," she said, "of being compared with Newton and Brookline. I'm tired of apologizing for living in Boston. What's the matter with Boston? When anybody moves out of the city he forgets he ever lived here. We're paying for half the suburban services. Every time my sister out there flushes the toilet it costs me more than it costs her. The suburbs couldn't care less."

Despite these inequities, Mrs. Nathanson is not certain that a metropolitan school district, which would prevent escape across the city lines, is a good idea; but she is persuaded that there has been too much emphasis on the problems of the disadvantaged and that Metco reflects it. "The Negro militants do not speak for many, many Negro parents. My Negro friends tell me that the civil rights groups don't represent them. They don't want to be spoken for. So much emphasis is placed nowadays on the disadvantaged and the very advantaged that there's a tendency to forget the millions in the middle."

But what shall be done about the millions in the middle? In Boston, theoretically, the Home and School Association should represent them—should represent them with devotion and energy. It is in a position to be the voice of the children and parents who have fallen between civil rights and the suburbs, the average middle- and lower-middle-class city dwellers who have chosen, or have been compelled, to remain in the core, the people increasingly fearful that their place—in Boston or Chicago or Detroit or even Englewood—is being squeezed between affluent exclusiveness and militant egalitarianism (and often by an alliance of the two), and who are expected to pay the price of fashionable liberalism by integrating *their* children in *their* schools. These are the people who, despite the merits of its good intentions, are the victims of the Racial Imbalance Law, a law directed not at regions but at school districts, and which penalizes biracial communities but exempts those which are exclusive or restrictive enough to exclude Negroes altogether. (In the fall of 1966 there were small signs of an incipient revolt among Irish parents in South Boston whose children, for the second consecutive year, were subject to double sessions in one South Boston elementary district. These parents had been promised mobile classrooms, but when schools opened they had not yet materialized. The protests were poorly organized, and they did not amount to much politically, but people close to Mrs. Hicks said that "she was acting rather nervous.") The people of the Home and School Association are those with the most to gain from genuine metropolitanism—why should Mrs. Nathanson have to pay every time her sister flushes her suburban toilet?—with the greatest stake in good education. But the Home and School

Association fails the best interests of its own constituency because it cannot distinguish between the interests of Beacon Street and the interests of the city and its children, and because it has not yet shed its fear of educational politics. There was a time—and clearly the Home and School Association is a creature of that time—when "good government" meant building barriers between education and political action, when teachers and schools required protection against the inroads of self-serving urban politicians. The byword in city after city was to "keep the schools out of politics." In fact, of course, the schools have never been out of politics, but the myth of the unitary system (theoretically serving all the children without regard to special interests) made professional school people into civic heroes in the eyes of parents' organizations and of others with a legitimate interest in good education. Thus the Home and School Association now regards every civil rights attack on the administration and School Committee as suspicious, a political assault on the prerogatives of administrators and teachers who, at all cost, must be kept out of controversy and political conflict. It is inconceivable that people like Mrs. Nathanson are cynically committed to the political *status quo*, that they care about the jobs of janitors or the hierarchical integrity of the ancient system. But they have not yet learned that education *is* a creature of political interest, and that every administration, every school board, represents *somebody* and some attitude, and that, more than anything else, the Boston administration, sustained by a public with only limited expectations of education, represents itself. Mrs. Nathanson and many other members of the Home and School Association have devoted years of work to fund drives, committee meetings, planning conferences, and the everyday concerns of the schools. But the more they work, the more they seem committed to the magnificence of the system, and the more they seem to resent attacks upon it. The schools are political creatures, and if the politics of good education are ignored then the politics of Beacon Street will govern. It is time that the parents of the city—not the absentee parents of private school children, but the parents of children who must be educated in the public schools—it is time that *those* parents raised a little hell.

* * *

The tragedy of Boston is that the best, the most earnest, the most intelligent efforts defeat themselves. The Racial Imbalance Law is directed to the wrong targets; the independent schools—even in the talking stage—to the wrong people; the busing programs to the wrong children and the wrong places. All of them represent diligent, sincere efforts to alleviate some of the city's most vexing problems; yet all of them, in a situation of incredible complexity, are likely to exacerbate the very problems they are supposed to solve. Edward J. Logue, the administrator of the Boston Redevelopment Authority, and others, have pointed out that the imbalance law has no "enduring prospect of success" because Boston is no more capable than other cities of solving the problem of racial imbalance by itself. The consequences of large-scale busing or large-scale redistricting, as Logue points out, "would only serve to accelerate neighborhood change, decrease the chances of neighborhood stability, and begin all over again the cycle of racial imbalance in predominantly white neighborhoods." This is not to say that there are not areas and schools where judicious changes could not increase integration *and* stabilize neighborhoods. The sociologist Robert J. Havighurst has pointed out that in Chicago limited school integration can successfully be achieved by carefully adjusting racial proportions in those neighborhoods where residents are sufficiently secure not to feel threatened by racial change. (Pettigrew learned in Boston that only one percent of the people his researchers interviewed objected to sending their children to schools where there are a few Negroes, 22 percent objected to having their children attend schools that were half Negro, and 64 percent would object to sending their children to schools more than half Negro.) The inadequacies of the imbalance law therefore do not exempt the Boston School Committee from the responsibility—legal certainly, and social, too—of attempting to adopt policies to reduce segregation within the limits of existing local situations, and of declaring their intention, which they have never done, of minimizing imbalance by whatever techniques seem most appropriate. By initiating limited integration in a number of schools, assuring the affected areas of those limitations, and simultaneously increasing educational quality and services—that is, by complying and protecting, too—the committee could make a great deal of progress in the racial issue, at least symbolic progress, and progress in morale.

It could then turn to educationally more important matters. (It would also legitimize its own position as a critic of the Racial Imbalance Law.) But to the committee, busing or redistricting for racial purposes—perhaps even for educational purposes—is the very essence of evil, something on which there can be no reasonable discussion.

At the same time, however, the policy of the Commonwealth of Massachusetts, with its Puritan righteousness, demands something that Boston by itself cannot accomplish. The city's schools are now 25 percent Negro; the elementary schools are 28 percent Negro, and the lower grades are over 30 percent Negro. Any insistence on arbitrary acts of balancing will merely accelerate imbalance, just as it has in other cities; and to demand balance in a community where the public schools may become predominantly Negro (the parochial schools, not affected by the law, are overwhelmingly white) is absurd. The imbalance law, moreover, asks of the poor white in the inner city what it does not ask of the rich white in the exclusive suburbs, except, perhaps, by the logic of prohibiting everyone, rich and poor, from sleeping under the bridge. Under the law every community is required to eliminate imbalance, but since there are few Negroes in the suburbs, the law has no practical effect. Because of these inequities, because it establishes race as the only criterion of balance, and because it is essentially directed at one community (Springfield, Cambridge, and Medford have a few imbalanced schools), the law—Eisenstadt and the State Board of Education to the contrary notwithstanding —may indeed be unconstitutional. It is, at any rate, inequitable, foolish, and self-defeating. Many whites in Boston—even those who don't really understand the law and don't care about it—sense this discrimination, sense it and resent it, and know that the old upper crust, whether on Beacon Hill or in the suburbs, is up to its old tricks again.

And the suburban whites, at least some of them, have sensed it, too, and have therefore committed themselves to Metco. They have heard Logue's message (Logue was one of the first in Boston to propose busing children to the suburbs), and they are willing, at least for the moment, and on a limited basis, to try it. Some of them feel that Metco may be only the first step toward more ambitious metropolitan arrangements, but they are not—for obvious reasons—willing to discuss that possibility in public. "Let's try this for a while and see how it works out," said a Metco advocate in Wellesley. "You never know what might happen."

But unless Metco expands into a full-scale metropolitan arrangement, a genuine regional school district, that effort, too, will be self-defeating. It will take the most motivated children (and will it be only Negro children?) out of the city schools, leaving a still greater concentration of social disease, a residue of accumulating problems—children from the most deprived families, from homes where the very idea of quality education is strange, and where the notion of busing children to schools twenty miles from home is regarded at best as unnecessary.

Concurrently Metco will tend to drain the city schools of the parental interest, the political pressure, and the civil rights militancy that they clearly need. At the end of a year of Metco—at the end of a millennium of Metco—the suburbs will still have better school systems than the city, will still be spared the social and cultural difficulties that beset the city. The kids that go from Roxbury and North Dorchester to Newton and Lexington will not bring the rats, the dilapidated houses, the welfare bills, the overhead of decrepit buildings and tattered textbooks. And only in limited ways can they bring back the new curricula, the bright buildings, the consciousness of high culture that the suburbs enjoy. They will be well-scrubbed, well-behaved, well-motivated children (people like the Wellesley protestors will make sure of that), not the truants or the schoolyard vandals. The problem children will remain, making the schools of the city that much more undesirable, and giving them that much more of an evil reputation.

The tragedy of Metco, of The New School for Children, even of Exodus itself, is that they are essentially middle-class projects appealing to middle-class people with middle-class ambitions and attitudes. Collectively they will assist certain parents and children now subject to inferior schools by providing a measure of choice not previously available. They offer, on a limited basis, a *way out*. (And isn't this what Exodus means?) They provide alternatives. But they do nothing for public education in Boston, and neither, indeed, does the imbalance law. The net result of these enterprises may well be further deterioration of the Boston system—new escape valves divesting the School Committee and the administration of their responsibility to provide quality urban education while sanctifying the committee in the political regard of its constituency, and while perpetuating the economic and educational inequities that caused the problems in the first place.

Where will the new ideas and the new resources come from? Who will help relieve the crowded classes, the beleaguered teachers, the harassed administrators? Who will provide the children that generate the excitement and the incentives? How can the suburbs export the expertise and the attitudes that generate good education, rather than merely exporting the finished product? Who will open the Boston system for fresh blood unseasoned by careful aging in the vats of the ancient hierarchy? And who is concerned about the poor whites—always discriminated against—and not merely the poor Negroes? What of the children of the Irish civil servants, the stevedores, the bus drivers, and the store clerks, what of the kids of the Italians of the North End or the Lithuanian immigrants of South Boston? What of the city's staggering tax base —a tax base burdened as heavily in the cause of public education as any in America? Who will save the city rather than merely rescuing a few of its neglected children?

The problem in Boston and in other cities is that escape is too easy, that the anger, the frustration, the civic fury that should and would manifest themselves are dampened by partial expedients and by the simple solution of a parochial school, a private school, or a move across the city lines. "The race issue," said a Boston reporter, "may save the insolvent parochial schools." The most concerned people—understandably—do not send their children to the city public schools at all. The great prep schools of the region, and the suburbs themselves, thrive on this concern, and even those most active in trying to improve the public schools—people with genuine interest in the city's education—often send their children elsewhere. Rather than capturing the schools, they attempt to capture the School Committee, and even while working for better education in the city they advise their friends to send their children elsewhere. They cannot be indicted for this—no one can be asked to sacrifice his children to some dim prospect of social betterment —but their dilemma and their response illustrate the problem, and demonstrate what makes the situation morally and socially so complex. The quandary of the concerned—people who passionately believe in public schools but who, nevertheless, send their children elsewhere—defines what may be the greatest tragedy in urban America today.

* * *

The Boston situation demands not merely reform or adjustment; it demands a fundamental revolution in political structure and educational practice. It demands a new style of school—a school open to the community, open at all hours and to all people, a school concerned not merely with apologizing for the going order and attempting to brainwash kids into some sort of passive acceptance (in the name of discipline, or manners, or morale, or patriotism), but one that seeks to reform that order and that identifies with the genuine problems of the people it proposes to serve. The school of the city—in all its practices and attitudes—must be based on an understanding of the society not as some static body of inherited and established relationships, but as a dynamic, dangerous, and often corrupt order, an order that cannot be comprehended on the basis of old pieties and maxims and that requires, more than anything else, tremendous social competence. This world demands a high level of cultural and academic skill: training sufficient for future retraining, and the understanding required to decide when that retraining becomes necessary, the political intelligence required for community action, and the sophistication to deal with the policemen, welfare clerks, housing inspectors, insurance peddlers, the promoters of "nothing down, forever to pay," and all the other forces that beset urban life. It demands, moreover, a sense of mastery, a belief that the world can be controlled, a confidence that even though the world is devious and complex it can be understood, and that such understanding can come through continual self-education and independent action. This, presumably, is what first-class citizenship really means. All formal guarantees of rights —without those skills and that confidence—are worthless.

Boston by itself cannot solve its problems, either in integration, or in education, or in finance; and neither can it be saved by fragmentary gestures from the suburbs. It lacks the money, the teaching personnel, the talented and motivated children. Concurrently the suburbs, their schools filled with children of almost identical background, lack the diversity to break down the smug ennui, the greenbelt isolation, and the privatist morality of their salubrious exclusion. ("We have problems, too," they all say, and in some measure they do; but the problems stem more often from the blight of narrow ambition and social isolation than from poverty or disease.) For them, as for the city, genuine integration means not merely some marginal busing program, hauling a few underprivileged kids across the city limits. It means a complete merger of resources and of concern. Suburbs without a central city are culturally effeminate clusters of homogeneity lacking the richness that gives meaning to the metropolis. The city without suburban talent and concern becomes a vast ghetto.

Boston, a core of under 700,000 in an urban region climbing toward three million, is an educational and social absurdity. It is too large and too rigid to invite genuine citizen participation and neighborhood action, too small to provide the social and economic base that quality education requires. The city, by taxing itself to the limit, manages to spend about two thirds as much per child for schools as Lincoln or Newton spend with ease. It cannot integrate racially nor socially nor economically. (And if it is desirable educationally to mix Negro and white children, then surely it is also desirable to mix rich and poor, Protestant, Catholic, and Jew, urban and suburban.) But the city schools have virtually no middle-class children, rarely enjoy the concern of middle-class parents, and, thus far, provide little to attract them.

Among the 2.5 million people in the Boston metropolitan area are some of the most talented, highly trained, highly sophisticated individuals in America. These are the people who not only have access to the outside culture and ideas; they produce the ideas, they *are* the culture. Without Harvard and M.I.T., without the Boston Symphony and the Massachusetts General Hospital, American society would hardly be the same. Thus the very things that make Boston tax poor also make it culturally rich, providing a base for what could be the most magnificent system of public education in America. Boston is not an isolated village in Nebraska, or some Appalachian hollow, far from the intellectual and cultural power that orients American life. It can capture that power and that talent—can enlist it, not by piecemeal demonstration projects, but by declaring its desire for new ideas and new life, for significant relationships with the universities and museums, and by freeing itself (or being freed through legislative action) from the irrational political limits that now bind it. Given these limits, and given the limited attitudes operating within them, only a genuine metropolitan school district can achieve the possibilities for relevant urban education. There is no existing model for such a district in any major city in America, no standard formula that communities can adopt and implement. The metropolitan idea for specific municipal functions is hardly new—Boston itself has several (for parks, water supply, and transportation)—but it is almost altogether novel in education, a public enterprise still subject to a great mystique of localism rarely borne out by the virtues of actual practice. Yet for Boston, hemmed in, decimated, and deprived, metropolitanism is a prime necessity. The city's situation and limitations offer few other reasonable alternatives.

A metropolitan Boston school district, based on a single property tax on city and suburbs, and serving both, would provide a central administration for personnel and recruitment, a common planning authority, centralized responsibility for new construction and maintenance, a common staff of specialists, and general responsibility for school operations, and for liaison with other institutions and organizations—universities, museums, orchestras, community groups, and the state and federal governments. It would eliminate inequities in the tax structure, reduce duplication of efforts, and make accessible to city and suburbs the best of the area's resources and talents. The district would also break the hold of the old Boston hierarchy and School Committee by giving suburban interests, through their population advantage, a dominant voice in the governing board of the new organization. This board, elected for long terms (say, six years) from separate geographical areas within the region—and therefore eliminating the biennial citywide school committee elections—would appoint a general superintendent responsible for the central administration, for the conduct of several regional 5,000-student campus high schools (some of them running through the fourteenth year for specialized training), for the operation of other specialized area schools (schools for the handicapped, for example), and for the general management of the system. Within the metropolitan structure, the district should be divided into neighborhood subdistricts each comprising some 50,000 people (about 10,000 school children) and each electing its own neighborhood school committee. The district committees would, in consultation with the central administration and local staff, have general authority over the local curriculum and educational policy, be empowered to conduct neighborhood programs and special educational and cultural activities, and be charged with general responsibility for supervising the operations of the local schools. Each would receive a standard per-pupil allocation of funds for materials and instructional facilities, and would be enabled, with the help of the central administration, to raise additional funds from individuals, foundations, business, and the state and federal governments. Each district might also be offered a small cash bonus for every pupil who, under open enrollment, chooses to enter its schools from another district. Such an incentive would help offset neighborhood fears of strange children (Negroes, poor kids, Italians) and add an inducement to make schools attractive to students from other parts of the region.

The metropolitan district would centralize all the responsibilities now diffused among different authorities, political subdivisions, and individuals. It would become responsible for integrating the schools—racially and socially—and thus, even when genuine integration is physically or geographically impossible, there would be no question of where power and authority rest. The district would have access to all the financial resources for public education in the area, and would be charged with sole responsibility for coordinated educational planning and development. More important, since many areas would, at least for the foreseeable future, remain racially and socially homogeneous, the organization of the district would give genuine meaning to the concept of the neighborhood school—giving the neighborhood, not the central administration, not the School Committee—a major voice in deciding what is taught, and how it is taught. It would give the immediate community a measure of participation it now lacks. It would provide a degree of academic pluralism—even a measure of internal competition—that the system could effectively use. It would enable the people of Roxbury, for example, to determine that they want more Negro history taught, or that they want to teach civics as prescribed by James Baldwin (that is, to teach reform rather than accommodation to the social order), or that they want (subject to financial limitations) more French and less business education. It would enable the individual district, not the central administration, to determine how federal funds for deprived area children are spent. It would give the community access to the performance records and other data for individual schools. It would make the neighborhood school—as long as it remains—a genuine community enterprise, not merely a political dodge for segregation.

There would, clearly, be checks on the subdistricts. The regional campus high schools, some with specialized academic and vocational programs, would exert an academic influence through their admission standards and educational techniques, much as the colleges now influence the secondary schools. Concurrently the curricular planners, if they are competent, would represent a body of expertise, a resource of information and advice, while the central staff itself, through its power to appoint teachers, would have substantial influence. But the greatest check, surely, will come in the competition between schools and districts, from the feeling in one neighborhood that the next has more relevant programs or textbooks or facilities. At the same time the several district committees would be powerful lobbies in the chambers of the central administration and the metropolitan school committee.

Will the city accept such a plan? Will the suburbs? The very fact that the suburbs exist, and that city and suburbs remain proudly contemptuous of each other indicates that acquiescence will be hard to achieve. And yet, even as little as three years ago, the ideas that led to Metco appeared entirely unacceptable even in the most progressive suburban circles. It had simply never occurred to anyone. Now there are people in Newton and Lexington and Brookline who feel that even Metco is insufficient, and that only a genuine metropolitan arrangement can solve the city's problems, and can provide the diversity and options that the smaller suburbs lack. The creation of a regional district has been proposed by the Boston Finance Commission, a semiautonomous committee appointed by the governor and responsible for general supervision of the city's financial activities. "A metropolitan district," the commission announced early in 1966, "would offer the possibility of correcting both the racial imbalance and fiscal imbalance which now plague

Boston and hamper its education efforts. . . . The metropolitan district would open up new educational opportunities for youngsters from smaller communities (who) often have no choice but the community's one high school. . . . A metropolitan district would allow the suburban communities to play their part in the resolution of a metropolitan problem and would encourage intercommunity cooperation. . . ." A metropolitan plan is clearly in the interests of the heavy taxpayers of the city—the bankers and real estate brokers, the insurance companies, and even the small homeowners of Dorchester, Jamaica Plain, and Brighton. It makes sense to anyone trapped by the inaction of the School Committee—by the subtle discrimination and the endless platitudes—and by the pathetic biennial spectacles called school committee elections. It is in the interest of the people genuinely concerned with civil rights, for only regional schools can integrate rich and poor as well as white and black. It is in the interest of a genuine regional plan for housing, transportation, and community services, for no plan that excludes educational facilities can possibly stand up. The federal government, pressed to develop new means of stimulating school integration—or at least of arresting the further deterioration of the central city, is likely itself to start offering incentives to suburban communities that initiate cooperative educational efforts with the neighboring central city (and clearly the government's support of Metco indicates at least a tentative interest). Under Title IV of the Elementary and Secondary Education Act, the government is already financing the creation of large, regional education "laboratories" formed through the collaboration of other institutions, devoted to experiment, innovation, and development, and likely soon to become major centers of educational power. There is no reason to believe that these institutions (one is being formed in the Boston area) will fail to stimulate even greater cooperative efforts, and give Washington greater incentives to finance them. Since the government is now under pressure from mayors, civil rights leaders, and other urban interests to develop programs to aid cities (and aid is being increasingly understood to involve schools as a prime element), the chances are good that experiments in metropolitan cooperation will receive—are already receiving— serious consideration.

All recent developments in education indicate a mounting

awareness that small districts are becoming increasingly irrelevant, undemocratic, and ineffective. All through the country, the various states are offering financial bait to small school systems to consolidate into larger units, eliminating overhead and providing sufficient pupils and money to support adequate educational programs. All through the country, cities have discovered that they cannot integrate alone. And all through the country, it is becoming clear that the cost of education—and especially the cost of the new educational technology—are prohibitive to small districts. The new possibilities of programmed and computer instruction, educational television, long distance xerography, and central cataloguing of library resources are producing fantastic possibilities for education. They make possible an increasing decentralization of learning situations while demanding, simultaneously, an increasing concentration in curriculum development, planning, and administration. The new techniques may well produce new categories of master teachers and planners, as well as a new breed of classroom leader, a man or woman trained in genuine process learning to work intensively with small groups of children. Through the options that these changes produce, a strong central system may be able to offer local teachers a far greater range of curricular choices. (If instructional materials can be transmitted by xerography from a central source, for example, then the long-term commitment to textbooks, and even paperbacks, is no longer necessary. A teacher can then request, on a day-to-day basis, documents, pictures, charts, and other resources that she could hardly afford now.) But all of these services demand centralization because only a large system, or a closely linked association of smaller systems, can collect the original material and afford the transmitting and reproduction devices to use it.

But for Boston—perhaps for other cities as well—the most persuasive reason for a metropolitan system lies simply in the facts of the existing situation. There will be no genuine public education in the city if the suburban populations remain perpetually exempt from the obligation to support it. There will be no substantial chance for improvement if the tax inequities, the racial inequities, and the social inequities continue. There will be no prospect of change if the old city hierarchy continues to control the schools for another generation. Boston, like other places, has already turned into a system of have-not schools, schools that are nothing but a network of holding and rescue operations—a perpetual crash program manned by semidesperate people, a dedicated minority, and an accumulation of timeservers. The future of the city, the entire meaning of the city, depends on its public facilities, and most notably on its schools. It is the schools that must become the center of redevelopment and long-range planning, and it is the educational program that lies at the heart of the schools. Too much of urban planning in America has been divorced from the substance of education and other cultural activities; too much has been physically and architecturally oriented. Until there is a plan for education—not merely for the construction of schools—there is no plan at all. And unless there is education, there will be no city.

AMERICA has developed a double system of public education, one half largely suburban, white, and middle class, the other urban (or remotely rural), often dark skinned, and usually poor. On the surface the two parts are similar: often their lists of courses, their organization, even, at times, their rhetoric, are identical. But they are not the same. One half leads from better homes, through brighter, well-financed schools, to colleges and universities, then on to the lucrative life in similar suburbs. The other takes children from depressed areas—the poor, the deprived, the oppressed— through dark and aging buildings, and then back to the slums from which they came. It adds little of cultural value, prevents the accumulation of social or economic resources, and leaves the next generation with no more than the last.

The two parts of the system are sufficiently well linked to enable one to drain the other—of children, teachers, and interest— but they are also sufficiently separated by a network of social valves and traps to prevent back up, to block flow in the wrong direction: no poor people to rich schools, no rich resources to poor schools. It is easy to distinguish the pauper schools from the others: they are the ones with the dark red brick buildings, the broken windows, the locked doors, the cramped schoolyards, and —often—the historic names: George Washington High School, the Theodore Roosevelt School, the John Marshall High School, the Oliver Wendell Holmes Junior High School, the Benjamin Franklin High School. If they are named for Negroes—Crispus

Attucks, George Washington Carver, Booker T. Washington—one invariably finds Negroes inside them. If their names include a compass direction they are usually in a new part of town, are themselves new, and have nothing but whites (Topeka West High School; Newton South High School; Alameda West High School). Anything with a spacious green periphery usually has a lily-white interior.

Segregation between the two systems—racial, economic, and social segregation—is growing. As the population of the core cities becomes more Negro (and Puerto Rican), as the suburbs grow and spread, the divisions between schools, and between systems, become ever more sharply defined. More than half the white urban population of America now lives outside the central cities; more than half the Negro population of all America lives inside. (By 1960, some 73 percent of all American Negroes lived in urban areas, four fifths of them in the central cities.) Simultaneously the schools—never really integrated—have become increasingly segregated, losing not only their white children, but also their middle-class interest and tax base. Negro migration into the northern cities, replacing the departing middle class, and the very public policy that was designed to foster integration have combined to accelerate segregation *between* systems. New York, Chicago, Philadelphia, and other urban centers have operated some predominantly Negro schools as long as they have had Negroes; but they also had a preponderance of white children from the middle class and the parental interest that accompanied them. Now it is not only certain schools that lack the parents and the interest (and the tax support), it is, ever more, entire systems. Public policy, clearly well intentioned, has accomplished the very opposite of what it was designed to achieve. Instead of integrating the schools it has segregated them all the more hopelessly. By insisting on racial balance more emphatically than it insisted on educational quality it has helped drive out the people required not only for racial integration, but for the maintenance of effective schools in the city at large. Washington's public schools are 90 percent Negro. They cannot possibly be integrated as they are now organized. Negroes now constitute half of Chicago's public school population and close to half of New York's. Philadelphia has a Negro majority, while the percentages in other cities are climbing. In New York the public schools are losing whites at the rate of 25,000 a year and gaining nonwhites at a rate of 36,000 a year; the schools of Manhattan are classified as 77 percent nonwhite. San Francisco, which had virtually no Negroes before World War II, now operates a system that is 25 percent Negro (in addition to large numbers of Oriental and Mexican Americans). In Cleveland and Detroit, in Newark and Milwaukee, segregation grows in step with, and often faster than, the Negro influx. "A Negro youngster in an American elementary school," said U.S. Commissioner of Education Harold Howe II recently, "has on the national average not much more than 15 percent of his classmates from the majority white groups. White high school students can expect nine of ten of their classmates from their own white groups." In Chicago and Philadelphia, 90 percent of the Negro children attend schools that are more than 90 percent Negro (the parochial schools are overwhelmingly white, as they are in Boston and almost everywhere else). In Los Angeles 77 percent of Negro children attend school in one of two districts. And in every city the suburbs remain largely white; in every city the white children attend a declining number of white schools.

The divisions are not merely racial; they are also social and economic. Segregation divides rich from poor, the culturally affluent from the socially deprived. Even the white children in the public schools of core cities are generally children of lower-middle-class families—families sometimes as deprived as those in the black ghetto, and as little able to raise the cultural and educational levels of the schools their children attend. At the same time the parental interest and middle-class motivation has moved to the suburbs, leaving behind the welfare burdens, the decaying plant, and the social overhead imposed by history and the growing poor. The city, with its shrinking tax capabilities, has been abandoned and left with responsibilities it cannot possibly discharge alone. (Although it could clearly do a great deal better than it has.)

To say that America has a double system of education is no longer just a metaphorical device or a statistical curiosity; it has become a political and geographical reality, and it is powerfully reflected in academic quality and performance. More and more, as segregation spreads, the city schools become holding operations for children with no place to go; more and more the educational process selects children out of the social mainstream before they have a chance to develop. Affluent education in the suburbs is a perpetual second chance well equipped with academic first aid and therapy, a continual opportunity for children to redeem themselves from previous academic or personal failure. There are few second chances in the cities—despite all the well-advertised rescue programs—because motivation, ambition, and confidence are crushed. Children who begin the first grade with enthusiasm drop out in the ninth; kids who score above average in reading in the second grade are two years behind in the seventh; children of six who instinctively understand that school is the first step from home to the larger world eventually learn through experience that the whole enterprise is a fraud, a hypocritical apology of the society and the system. They internalize official opinions about their own shortcomings, making it necessary, as one social worker said, "to debrainwash them" before they can ever be reclaimed. These are not merely Negro children—they can be children of every race —but proportionately there are, among them, far more Negroes and Puerto Ricans than any others. White kids can identify with the symbols of social success—on television, in the magazines, in the newspapers; they are not constantly reminded of their inferiority by the patronizing attitudes of teachers, cops, and welfare workers, and they have long learned that, whatever the state of their homes or families, they are at least a notch or two above the colored in the next neighborhood. For the Negro kids, with no other psychic resources, the consequences are far more damaging. These are the children who often prefer the security of segregation to the frustration of competition and life "outside," who have come—through irrational fear, or through well-founded experience —to regard the world beyond the immediate neighborhood as alien and incomprehensible. In Boston a 17-year-old dropout misses an opportunity to join the Women's Job Corps because she doesn't know how to find the local office and is afraid to ask; in San Francisco, high school students confess that they have never seen the Pacific Ocean. Many of them are children with peasant attitudes, the fears and suspicions of small villagers who have never traveled beyond their little corner of the earth, and who have seen only the underside of life. To them things like the formalities of the Constitution of the United States or the rules of English grammar are less than meaningless because nothing in their experience provides any link with the official world. Even the life of the larger city in which they live, the life of buses and subways, of employment offices and expense accounts, of museums and music, is a compound of rumor, imagination, myth, and fantasy. Many of these children can cope with frustrations and problems that would paralyze well-heeled suburbanites—how to deal with rats or evade the imperious questions of officialdom, how to manage without breakfast or sleep despite the noise of family brawls and the relentless chatter of the television set—but their connection with the visible culture of success, mobility, complexity, and change is at best tenuous.

This is not to say that all Negro children live in tenements, that they are all unmotivated, or that they all come from broken homes. Part of the exasperation of every urban Negro community is that it has popularly been associated with welfare, social breakdown, delinquency, and crime. "You know," said a Negro mother in Boston, "many of us do live in decent apartments, read books, feed our children breakfast and buy them good clothes. Sure, there's places with rats and broken windows and garbage in the halls, but don't think that everybody lives that way." Nevertheless, it is clear that the incidence of social dislocation in the ghetto is dramatically higher than it is elsewhere in the society. The unemployment rate for nonwhite males in urban areas (1960) stood at 9.3 percent, a little over double that for whites; the median income for Negro families (1963) was $3,465, about half the median for whites. The Department of Health, Education, and Welfare has estimated that 60 percent of all Negro children growing up in America today are living in what the department considers poverty-stricken families. "At any moment," wrote Daniel P. Moynihan, then Assistant Secretary of Labor, "some 36 percent of Negro children are living in homes where one or both parents are missing. It is probable that not much more than one third of Negro youth reach eighteen having lived all their lives with both parents."

The schools these children attend are, like their pupils, among the most deprived and the most burdened in America. Boston's Irish hierarchy, its meager tax resources, its segregation, its rigidity—all these things are only extreme and particular examples of a national condition. "This city," said a Bostonian ironically, "is not typical of anything except itself." And yet, in most respects, the financial and social problems repeat themselves in almost every major city in America. Although recent pressure from civil rights groups has generated attempts to produce parity in the measurable indices of public education (book allocations, teacher salaries, teacher-pupil ratios), the discrepancies continue. In Chicago, for example, the U.S. Commission on Civil Rights learned that the total appropriation per pupil in the white elementary schools (in 1962) was $342 while that for the Negro schools was $269, that the percentage of uncertified teachers in Negro schools (49 percent) was quadruple that of the white schools, that the average number of pupils per classroom was almost 47 in Negro schools, compared to 31 in white schools. In Harlem, the percentage of novice teachers—teachers with three years' experience or less—is more than double the city average (42 percent against 20 percent); in Milwaukee the percentage of inexperienced teachers in the core schools is about 20 percent higher than the city average; in Detroit one of four teachers in certain slum schools is an emergency substitute working on a regular assignment; in Chicago some schools are unable even to get substitutes for absent teachers, and have pressed librarians and others into "temporary" service on an all-but-regular basis; in Topeka, Kansas, the children in the all-Negro junior high school must buy their lunch and milk outside while white kids in modern cafeteria-equipped schools get theirs under federally subsidized programs. In the metropolitan areas of the northeast, according to a recent U.S. Office of Education survey, 40 percent of Negro children attend high schools more than 40 years old (as compared to 15 percent of the whites); these schools have a median of 35 children per room (28 for whites), and they offer each student fewer resources—language laboratories, library books—than their white counterparts. In city after city the Negro schools are the most poorly equipped, the oldest, and the most crowded. Their teachers are ill trained for work in the slums; the facilities, dating from an older era, are inadequate; and their buildings are decaying, remnants of several ages of neglect. Most important, perhaps, is the fact that the teachers—and the system they serve—are conditioned by attitudes as archaic as the buildings in which they work. Intuitively they associate clean clothes with good minds, pleasant manners with academic success. Having learned to value classroom order above everything else, they relegate rebelliousness, rudeness, and unfriendly curiosity to the netherworld of "alienation," "unteach-ability," and incipient crime. Those who try to be sympathetic often manage only to be patronizing ("I feel for those poor children") and those who do not have often given up, waiting only for the next opening on the transfer list. They have heard about cultural deprivation and have learned to use it as a cover for their own confusion, pointing to the home, the community, the surrounding squalor as the prime causes for educational failure. "The tendency on the part of some educators, and others, to lump all children in a racial ghetto as 'culturally deprived' and therefore uneducable," said the Negro psychologist Kenneth B. Clark, "is an insidious form of stereotypic thinking and is a contemporary version of the earlier versions that Negroes are innately inferior. The educational effects of the arguments for cultural inferiority are the same as the earlier and more primitive assertions of racial inferiority. Both points of view lead to the development and implementation of educational procedures which stunt the ability of the child to learn and result in the self-fulfilling prophecy that he does not learn. If it is assumed that a child cannot learn, and if he is treated as if he cannot learn, he will not learn." In most instances, teachers in ghetto classrooms expect little, and get little in return. Their contempt often is ill-disguised, reinforcing what the kids already suspect—that the whole enterprise is a cruel formality that signifies nothing. "I'm not here because I like it," a teacher told a Chicago high school class. "As soon as I can I'm going to transfer to a white school." In Harlem a white teacher told interviewers:

> They (the teachers) give up too easily. Give up before they get started. Don't have sufficient interest. The teachers throw children out of their classes or simply just stop teaching them. They put work on the board and let it go at that. . . . Some teachers ask for the worst classes because they don't have to work. In the worst classes they don't have to work because whatever happens, they can just say, "It is the children."

Even in the better schools, where there are no policemen patrolling the halls, where the rooms are bright and the windows unbarred, the teachers, afflicted by subtle despair, conduct classroom charades in which the children pretend to learn and the teacher pretends to believe them. The kids parrot back the textbook clichés, meaningless phrases about Eskimos and Indians, about *i* before *e* (except in neighbor and weigh), and about the friendly policeman (the same one who shakes down the numbers runners), participating in an endless series of recitations, and unrelieved monologues that slavishly follow a syllabus prepared for someone else in another age. That, for the teacher, is the safest thing to do. It requires little effort or imagination, and it produces results no worse than the average. Adherence to the rule book is always the best line of defense.

There are, of course, magnificent teachers and principals— people who battle their own school boards and administrations in behalf of the children they are assigned to teach. In New York an elementary principal joins the picket line in front of his own school to demonstrate for better facilities; in San Francisco a teacher goes from home to home exorting parents to support their children in school activities and help them with their work; in Chicago teachers quietly abandon the required syllabus and work long hours to develop programs relevant to the lives and interests of their students. But these people operate in defiance of, not in conformity with, the system. They break the official rules, contend with the established administration, and violate the standards that are supposed to guide them. They identify with the children rather than with hierarchy, and they sometimes jeopardize their own careers in doing it. "I hope you're not from the Board of Education," said a Chicago teacher to a visitor as he distributed leaflets published by a civil rights organization to a remedial reading class. "If they knew I was using this stuff instead of the adopted manual I'd probably get fired."

The consequences of these systems are everywhere apparent. In almost every city, as in Boston, the children of the ghetto dominate the statistics of educational failure—and the statistics themselves are merely polite euphemisms for a mounting accumulation of human disaster. Each year—in New York, in Boston, in Chicago, in Detroit, in Cleveland—they fall farther behind the norms. In New York City, the average sixth grader is reading roughly on a par with other sixth graders in the United States, but in Central Harlem he is an even two years behind; in the all-Negro schools of Roxbury he is a year and a half behind; in the South side of Chicago he is a year and a half behind. At the same time, it is the core city kids—and especially the Negroes—who lead the dropout rates: the chances of a ghetto child completing high school are about even—half never make it. In the suburbs the chances are about nine in ten. The average white child in the year 1967 will attend school from one to two years longer than the average Negro.

In recent years we have learned something, however, that may turn out to be even more significant: differences in the performance of children *within* schools are as great as the differences between schools. Cultural disadvantage dogs a child, it seems, no matter where he attends school. What this suggests, of course, is not that we can shift the responsibility for academic failure to the parents or the home, but that the schools do a great deal *less* than anybody thinks they do. To put it another way, where education depends entirely on the school, it turns out pretty badly; success comes from those situations in which the home environment, or some other external factor, provides the motivation, the discipline, and the interest. If this is so, then—at best—the schools do no more than magnify and amplify tendencies determined by outside influences; at worst they are simply irrelevant, not merely to the deprived—but to *all* children. Those who learn, would learn regardless of the school. The logic is fairly simple: either the schools can educate (or, better, can get children to learn) or they can't. And if they can succeed only with those bound to succeed, then they need to be reformed from the top down. In education, as in almost everything else, the customer is always right. When half of Harlem or of Roxbury fails, then it is the schools that need adjustment, not the kids.

Urban education in America is increasingly becoming Negro education; it already has become—in general, and with notable exceptions—education for the lower-middle class. At the same time, and despite much rhetoric to the contrary, it still remains rooted in the suppositions and attitudes of the small town. It presumes, for example, that children will come to school with values and skills corresponding to those of Noah Webster's Spelling Book, Ben Franklin's aphorisms, and to the general gospel of success. It is oriented to the notion that everyone has a mother and father, not merely for administrative convenience, but also for the purposes of personal identity. It still conceives (in its textbooks, the spellers, and readers—and in the foundations of classroom discourse) of "normal" life as something surrounded by a lawn and a picket fence. It still regards the neighborhood as something organic, yet stable, a perpetual source of social value and identity; and it regards the unitary school and the unitary classroom—even in this age of mass communications—as the essence of education. It still acts, despite the corruption and miseries of the cities, and of much else in contemporary life, as if it must eulogize the social system, as if reality were defined by the Declaration of Independence, the small shop, and the farm. Time after time it manages to confuse children through its attempts to link contemporary figures with the mythology of the past, a semidesperate manipulation of observed behavior to fit the formulas of ancient tradition. In their brilliant description of Harlem schools, published under the title of *The Schoolchildren,* Mary Frances Greene and Orletta Ryan quote a fourth grader:

> George Washington comes in a little closer; he knows his father gonna whup him, but he say "Excuse me, sir. I done it. I cannot tell no lie. I am like Martin Luther King."

What is really relevant about Martin Luther King is not that he is honest—in the ghetto, honest people finish last—but that he is a revolutionary who understands that the going system is lousy, and who has learned how to fight it. He appeals because he has managed to restore to thousands of Negroes—often vicariously—a small semblance of hope and dignity, and because he has demonstrated at least the possibility of mastering the system, and of altering it. It was not done through honesty, but through a great deal of skill, courage, and defiance. King is a great man because he changes things, not because he accepts them.

The urban school is isolated. Located in the midst of change, in close physical proximity to all forces of the society—to revolution in the slums and in technology, to the universities and industry, to politics and government—it behaves, administratively and pedagogically, as if it were somewhere in the middle of Siberia, or in a rural hamlet of self-sufficient farmers. It is distant both from the contemporary world and from the people and community it presumes to serve, and it spends a great deal of energy inventing devices to maintain that distance. No one can enter a school in Boston after classes begin without ringing the bell at the locked door (to protect the children, it is said, from molestation and disturbance). In Chicago the telephone numbers of individual schools are kept unlisted, a closed, dark secret to protect the principals from the people; in an emergency a parent can reach his child only by relaying the message through the downtown headquarters. In both cities the much-proclaimed decentralization (in which separate areas are placed under the jurisdiction of district superintendents) simply adds another administrative barrier between the neighborhood, the local school, and the people who make the real decisions downtown. In system after system, the concept of community involvement means—at best—that the locals are invited to meetings where they can express their views; usually it only means that, in return for a cookie and a glass of punch, they have the privilege of being told what they are doing wrong at home, and how they should instill the proper attitudes in their children. With federal funds and other special resources New York and other cities are opening some schools early and keeping them open at least until 6 P.M., so that children can play, or participate in special classes, tutoring programs, and recreational activities. But in most cities the buildings are still shutting down at three, not to open again until next morning, or Monday morning, or the Monday after vacation. While community groups beg landlords and ministers for space to conduct tutoring programs, while they meet in old storefronts and church basements, the school administrators express their regret, but they just don't have the resources, or the authority, or the janitors, to keep the buildings open. In the meantime—in Chicago, in Boston, in New York—the teachers have departed for their moonlight jobs, their suburban residences, or to some night school where they can pick up a few more credits to qualify for another increase in pay. Some, of course, work late hours preparing for class, attending meetings, calling on parents, and tutoring children on their own time, but most of them do it despite the systems in which they work, do it without reward or credit, and with only a dim suspicion on the part of their colleagues and superiors that they are bucking for a promotion, or are embarrassing the system by pandering to interests and concerns not defined in the rule book. "Standing apart from the community they serve," said former Commissioner of Education Francis Keppel, "these slum schools slammed their doors shut at three-thirty when school closed for the day; thus the school was presumably 'protected' from the neighborhood. In such schools, where the child was considered ungifted, the most dangerous gap in our society was permitted to grow and enlarge." Keppel wrote—for purposes of historical permanence—in the past tense, but the situations he describes have hardly changed at all. Outside of class hours, most urban schools are closed most of the time to most of the people.

Isolation, however, is not merely physical but political, ideological, and moral. What Keppel calls "the fortress school" reflects an attitude toward the community and toward the children, a basic conviction that, on the whole, the community is hostile to the school and that, if allowed too much access or control, it will destroy it. And, in part, that conviction is true. It is true not only because neighborhood vandals find school windows especially appealing, or because in some slums the teachers must always keep their desks locked to prevent pilfering, or because those same teachers get their tires slashed in slum area parking spaces, or because—with the justification of experience—they must escape the neighborhood before dark in order to be safe from attack, but also, and more fundamentally, because the school has never demonstrated that it is of any value to the people it serves, has proven, rather, that it is a device for selecting people out, for closing doors, and for establishing with all the impact of its official status that the children who attend are somehow benighted, second class, and inferior. The slum school—whether it is Forestville North in Chicago, or the Campbell in Boston, or any of a number prefixed P.S. in New York—is like the encampment of a foreign power, a potentate who claims to be able to qualify the colonial children for useful service in his own higher civilization and then, time after time, rejects them as unfit. His civilization—as demonstrated by the level of goods and services of the average citizen—is clearly superior; therefore it is the barbaric backwardness of the local people, not his school, that makes them unfit for elevation. The school rarely identifies with the community and, because it feels it must defend the society which created it, it manages to insult its own clientele for failing to live up to the accepted standards.

At the same time the school and the system which operates it disregard the realities of life outside the ghetto. Administrators speak perpetually about teaching children to live in the contemporary world, running on without end about "our changing society," the "technological revolution," the "process-centered learning," "independent study," "child-centered education," and "the needs of the modern world." In schools like the Bronx High School of Science and in innovative systems, like Pittsburgh's, the cities have attempted to develop significant programs and to work out new approaches. The Pittsburgh schools, for example, have collaborated with Carnegie Tech in the trial and implementation of an inductively oriented course in history and they are making other major efforts to upgrade public education sufficiently to stop the rush to the suburbs. A number of systems in the Cleveland area have jointly drawn up a new mathematics program. Seattle is seriously contemplating a major restructuring of its entire educational system, relying on campus schools, nongraded programs, and other devices to break down geographical and academic rigidity. Minneapolis is experimenting with a storefront school for potential junior high school dropouts who have learned to associate regular school buildings with educational and personal failure. Rochester, through a "lighted school" project centered in churches and community facilities, is conducting family instruction programs where parents are taught to read to their children, and where adults, volunteers, and children work together after school hours to raise the cultural aspirations of the community. But for the most part the language of reform—in the cities and elsewhere—reveals little comprehension of what innovation actually means, nor does practice betray any substantial change from the village pattern. Most of the billion dollars expended during the first year of the federal Title I program (for culturally disadvantaged schools) went to limited pilot programs and demonstration projects. Little of it was ever utilized with the intention of generating fundamental reforms, or of finding universal techniques, curricula, and modes of organization that would serve entire systems. Everywhere the money was used for patchwork, for small repairs, remedial programs, and for providing a few extra services—that is, for doing a little more of the same. Rarely did it go toward the initiation of changes that would recognize the realities of urban life, take advantage of new technology, or that would tend to shake the cozy routines of established practice.

Innovation and new courses, in most instances, do not appear downtown but on the periphery and in small cities. When the new physics course developed by the Physical Science Study Committee at M.I.T. was introduced, it was the suburbs, not the cities, that rushed to adopt it. Newton tried it, and Lexington tried it, and Jefferson County, Colorado, tried it, but Boston did not. As late as 1964, some six years after PSSC first came along, Chicago had probably no more than ten teachers who were trained to use it. In New York, which had sent a number of teachers to PSSC summer institutes, only a handful were actually using it. When Educational Services, Inc., now developing new programs in elementary and secondary social studies and English, tries out new materials, it generally does so in Newton or Lexington, not in Boston. When a completely nongraded school appears—allowing all students to proceed at their own levels in every subject—it appears in Melbourne, Florida, not in Chicago or San Francisco. When experimental schools are developed to provide ideal facilities for team teaching—employing clusters of rooms that can be joined or separated through movable partitions—they are built in suburban Colorado, in Southern California, even in the middle of small-town Kansas, not in any one of those supposedly urbane, cosmopolitan centers that make up the core cities. In the cities, somehow, the cumbersome hierarchy, the overhead of an aging plant, and the civil service detachment of teachers and staff, make change slow and painful. Chicago, for example, reviews each part of the curriculum every four or five years. In the interim—even when a teacher desires it—reform or innovation are all but impossible. When books or materials are ordered, they represent an academic and financial commitment that must be honored for years in classroom use. And even when changes are made, they generally represent merely an updating of the same old material taught according to existing methods: the curriculum review committees, whether in Chicago or Boston, are composed of senior teachers and administrators, people who have been brought up through the ranks and who are not likely to be rebels or innovators. Rare is the school department that gives new, young teachers a determining voice in curricular policy; and rarer still the one that is willing to seek out the revolutionaries outside the system to help design new programs. The cities have learned the fashionable rhetoric of innovation, but few of them practice it, except in the most peripheral fashion. They speak change but don't understand it, preach relevance but can't achieve it. As systems they remain oddly isolated from the social and intellectual currents that surround them—the dinosaurs of the urban world. "There is a difference," said a school superintendent recently, "between the horseless carriage and the automobile. But most school administrators haven't discovered it."

* * *

The city schools are at the crossroads of three revolutions—in civil rights, in technology, and in the style of urban life itself. All three are making fantastic demands upon education, and all three must be accommodated through an awkward political process that has never been efficient, even in the best of circumstances. The Negro revolution has put urban education on the social map, just as Sputnik helped draw attention to education in the suburbs and through the country generally. The focus of civil rights militancy has been on the schools: they have been the prime northern targets of the boycotts, the pickets, the legal processes, and the other major thrusts of the civil rights movement because they stand at the very center of Negro aspirations. They represent not only integration and some recognition of political and personal dignity, but they also offer the best, and perhaps the only, means of escape from historic deprivation and discrimination. In a sense, inadequate education has helped legitimize discrimination (and vice versa) and thus the schools have become the crucial institutions in the attempt to break the old cycle of futility and repression. It is no longer possible to rise by staking out a quarter section on the prairies, or by opening a small shop with no capital, or by doing favors for the immigrants in the wards. For the Negro, education appears to be the only way up.

At the same time, however, the demands for change and amelioration are confused. What is represented as "civil rights pressure" is in fact a series of disjointed, complex, and often contradictory recommendations. There is no single Negro demand for education, no agreement on what constitutes cultural disadvantage, not even agreement that the phrase means anything that can usefully be applied. In every community there is what someone has called "a coterie of automatic liberals," people both black and white who insist that integration and equality constitute the only basis for a long-term solution to the problem of inadequate Negro education. But what is genuine equality for children who lack the social and economic background to begin school on a par with white middle-class kids? What is parity for children who confront situations at home and in the neighborhood that place them at an automatic disadvantage in the classroom? How can one provide genuine education to children who come to school without breakfast, without sleep, and without the opportunity to do the homework, the reading, the traveling that other families take for granted? Concurrently, how can one overcome the restrictions of space and time (not to mention politics) that make genuine physical integration all but impossible? How does one integrate a system that is already 85 percent Negro, or one where the concentrations of whites and Negroes are so far separated by time and distance as to make wholesale busing or redistricting all but absurd? How does one arrest the exodus of whites from schools that approach the tipping point (usually around 25 or 30 percent Negro)? The difficulty of resolving these questions has strengthened the conflicting, and politically more acceptable, case for improving ghetto schools and for providing large doses of compensatory education. John H. Fisher, President of Teachers College, Columbia University, recently wrote that "even though supporting better schools in ghettos has become a favorite ploy of the advocates of separate equality, that fact does not justify neglecting ghetto children. Indeed many of these children are already so badly victimized by deprivation and neglect that, if integration were instantly possible, strong remedial and compensatory programs would still be necessary to give them any reasonable chance to compete or succeed." Compensatory education, it is said, strikes at the very heart of the problems of the disadvantaged child. It provides the services, the special attention he needs. It is tailored for his condition. But compensatory education also implies—almost as a necessity—some degree of segregation, either within schools or between schools, since those who are now being called "non-disadvantaged" children presumably don't need it. It also carries with it a certain tone of condescension, a patronizing quality that school administrators can exude with a particularly offensive air. People like Kenneth Clark properly criticize the concept of cultural disadvantage as a polite excuse for the ineffectiveness of the schools, as a shift of responsibility from the classroom to the family and the child. At the same time other critics—educational sociologists like Frank Riessman, for example—have accumulated evidence that cultural disadvantage really does mean something, and that the engines of education—tests, books, teachers, curricula —fiercely discriminate against children reared on experiences and language that have little in common with those taken for granted in middle-class schools. Almost all the existing preschool programs —programs like the federally financed Head Start—are premised on concepts of cultural deprivation, and particularly on the ideas of Martin P. Deutsch, a theorist in the field of developmental psychology who pointed out that the slum child may come to school with an aural conditioning that has taught him not to listen to anything but shouted one-word instructions. In New York, almost a decade ago, Daniel Schreiber demonstrated in the Higher Horizons Program that through small classes, cultural enrichment, and other devices, a school can raise the I.Q. scores of deprived children by as much as thirty points; similar effects have since been demonstrated elsewhere. But all these programs tend to segregate. Tracking segregates. Remedial reading segregates. Special schools segregate. At the same time Higher Horizons has also cast doubt on the possibilities of special cultural enrichment programs when they are extended to large numbers of schools, and when the original enthusiasm wears off. In its latter years Higher Horizons seems to have had almost no impact and, in 1966—after almost a decade of fanfare and publicity—it was quietly dropped. It demonstrated, more than anything else, that what can be done by a small, dedicated group in a demonstration project cannot always be applied on a large impersonal basis across the board. It illustrated the fallacy of the pilot program and the weakness of perfunctory "enrichment."

Because of the failures of efforts like Higher Horizons, and because of the large ratio of ballyhoo to performance in other pilot programs, even the moderate Negro leadership is properly suspicious of compensatory education, cultural enrichment, and the other standard gambits used by urban schools in response to critics; too often compensatory education has become an alternative to integration or to a general upgrading of the schools, and too often it has been a piecemeal, ineffective excuse for genuine action, a paper program which disappears before it ever reaches the child. Marvin Rich, one of the leaders in CORE's educational program in New York, flatly told a group of school administrators in Washington recently that "most enrichment programs fail." As they were congratulating themselves on their little pilot programs with disadvantaged children, he reminded them that Higher Horizons also had bright beginnings, that most special projects "are just additive." "You have to look at the entire system," he said. "You can't simply add to it and expect it to change." The problem is: what changes can be made, and what changes should be made? What does the Negro require of the schools—indeed, what does any child require?

In confronting these questions the American civil rights leadership is caught in a vicious cultural and political trap. Since few Negro leaders (and few other Americans) appeal to economic class interests, or even recognize their existence, they must presume to speak for all Negroes, rich and poor, and must pretend, for these are the rules of our political rhetoric, that all are respectable citizens with latent ambitions just awaiting fulfillment. Thus if the civil rights leadership insists that Negro children are no different from all others, and that Negro families, though poor, are just as interested in education as their white counterparts across town, then it cannot demand anything more than integration and equality. Given these premises it cannot argue that education in the public schools is irrelevant for Negroes (without arguing that it is also irrelevant for whites) and it must then produce the motivated children, the clean clothes, the decent behavior, and the bourgeois aspirations on which the public schools have always relied. If, on the other hand, it insists that, because of historic deprivation and existing inequities, Negroes have special problems, then it must be willing to accept—or even demand—some sort of special treatment for their children, treatment that inevitably implies segregation or differentiation.

Essentially the whole notion of integration *is* a liberal, middle-class idea. It appeals to middle-class Negroes and middle-class whites—to the northern NAACP and to the Urban League, rather than to CORE and to the more militant organizations. It appeals to people like the leaders of Exodus in Boston, and to the suburbanites who support them. It appeals to all those who prefer accommodation to conflict in the solution of social issues, and who want to use, rather than alter, the existing order in their climb to power and status. It does not appeal to those who see attempts at accommodation as futile, who regard integration in the cities as an impossible delusion, who judge middle-class public school programs and attitudes as irrelevant, and who assess the condition of the American Negro as sufficiently distinct from white society to require special solutions and new tactics in achieving them. Many people in the civil rights movement are ambivalent about the two positions, are unsure of the implications of "black power," and are, therefore, unable to resolve the cross-complexities of class, race, and politics. But they do know that so far integration has been a dismal failure; even those, who, like Kenneth Clark, are committed to it, recognize that interim solutions must be found in compensatory education and in upgrading the general quality of all-Negro schools. And many more are coming to the position that integration may not only be a failure in the short run, but that the prospects are dim even in the distant future. In some circles school integration is almost a dead issue, a bitter residue of yesterday's battles that will not be raised again. There have been few vocal demands for large-scale integration in the past two years, and almost no recent boycotts and demonstrations—except those directed to neighborhood control of segregated schools. In almost all the cities where Negroes constitute a significant proportion of the population the strategists are beginning to discuss not integration, not moral persuasion, but the capture of political institutions—city councils, school boards, and other public bodies—as the best way of achieving recognition and power. "The Negroes are going to follow the path of the Irish," said a white sociologist who has been associated with many of the major civil rights movements in America. "They're going to take over the big cities. Integration is just a device to drive the whites out a little faster. They've given up on integration. That's just the talk of the automatic liberals. The Negro militants are interested in power. Myrdhal made just one mistake. He talked about the dilemma between our racial practices and our professed beliefs. But we don't really even believe in integration."

The conflicting demands for integration and compensatory education, the fears of the remaining urban whites, and the deprived and sometimes hostile clannishness of those who live in the ghetto batter the schools in an endless series of waves, leaving them in a continuing state of paralytic shock and in postures of administrative defensiveness that have little success either in resolving the political conflicts of the community or in eliminating the educational weaknesses of the classroom. The remaining urban whites who send their children to the public schools are unable to join the Negro militants in a concerted campaign to upgrade education for all children: often they appear on the scene only to resist Negro demands for busing or redistricting, regarding the schools as the prime wedge for new Negro incursions into heretofore closed neighborhoods. They do not see that the paralysis of the system affects their schools as well, and they do not, on the whole, consider education with the same urgency as the Negroes. To the urban white the neighborhood school is a lever of security: no matter how poor, it is probably better than the Negro schools, certainly better than the same school with Negroes in it, and therefore a barrier against threats from below. As a consequence, the whites, like the system itself, react rather than lead, resist rather than initiate. They represent the backbone of the *status quo* in the city.

But they do not represent all of it. A substantial proportion of the Negro community feels just the way they do. In city after city it has been established that a sizable number of Negro parents—if not a majority—are equally reluctant to send their children out of the neighborhood, equally reluctant to see them go to school with children of other races, and of differing social backgrounds. This is a fact that has been used time and again by people like Louise Hicks to prove that Negroes (like Italians or Irishmen) "want to stay with their own kind," but their use of it to maintain segregation does not diminish its importance. At the heart of the ghetto lies a cautious and conservative spirit, a large and silent group of people who are politically inert, who have long come to accept limited possibilities and uncomplaining accommodation as the basic conditions of life, and who know that attempts to move very far, socially or geographically, result in humiliation and defeat. To them the ghetto represents security in an incomprehensible world: they know its horrors and its brutality, but better the familiar evils of the slum than the unknown dangers of the world outside. The passivity of such families, passivity reinforced by the desperate conditions of life and the precarious stability of the family, stands in odd contrast to the vocal leadership, to the legal and political militancy exhibited at school headquarters, and to the literature of the protest organizations. In fact, the children represented by the civil rights leadership in its appeal for better education often bear little resemblance to those who actually come to school. Many of them are not burning with ambition and motivation, and some are tough little rascals even before they set foot in the classroom. They are adept at deception, know how to defy the agents of officialdom, have already learned how to play the wily games of the slums. This is not to excuse the failures of the schools, or the contributory negligence of the educational hierarchy, but it does help explain the incredulity of the official response to the representations of the organized civil rights spokesmen. The children and the families those spokesmen are talking about are not the children the teachers see, and the problems so graphically described by CORE and the NAACP are rarely those most visible in the classroom. Daniel Moynihan has pointed out that demands for opportunity are founded on what he calls the Jewish model—on a presumption that given liberty to move ahead, the Negro will move ahead. But, he suggests, the Negro usually follows the pattern of the Irish: he is often a rural immigrant to the large city, a peasant unfamiliar with urban ways, and he therefore displays all the symptoms of social trauma (drunkenness, crime, and family breakdown) that the Irish displayed a century ago. Under these conditions, he says, one cannot expect the Negro to display the strong upward pressures, the motivation to climb, that the Jews displayed at the turn of the century. Whether or not his assessment is correct, it is clear that in drawing attention to the inadequacies of the city schools, the leaders of the civil rights movement have portrayed families and children who represent only a portion of the population that lives in the urban ghetto. Only rarely have they confronted the problems that the teachers actually see, and only rarely have they discussed the children they actually teach. Although they have pointed up—were, indeed, the principal voices in pointing up—the terrible shortcoming in urban education, they also helped confuse the issue because they have never been sure themselves what they wanted, or how they wished to get it.

* * *

Urban education is not merely a matter of civil rights, of Negroes, or of academic inequality. It lies at the very heart of the city's agony, constitutes its biggest planning liability, and its greatest debit for the future. Its inadequacies have helped make the city a community of the old, the rich, and the poor. It has contributed to the decay of the public interest and to the concomitant decline of related public facilities, and it has helped turn places like Chicago and New York into renaissance cities, complete with baronial high-rise palaces, private body guards, multiple locks, and, after sundown, vacant streets and vacant parks. The princes of these cities, while publicly decrying the state of their facilities, are able to isolate themselves from the surrounding squalor, to buy the private pleasures, the culture, and the education that should be accessible to all, which, after all, are the reasons for the city's existence, but which are available only to the few. What would happen to the schools of New York, for example, if the editors of the *New York Times*, the managers of the Chase Manhattan Bank, the owners of Macy's, if all the executives and painters and artists and intellectuals, if the admen and the television producers—if all of them *had* to send their children to those schools?

The schools of the city did not, of course, create its problems. But rather than helping to solve them, they have made them worse. Where they should be centers of community interest and activity they have become locked prisons with barred windows and obscenity-covered walls. Where they should be magnets to the concerned and the cultivated they have become repellents. Where they should be forces of neighborhood integration and cohesion, they have become sources of division and conflict. Not all city schools are prisons, not all offer substandard programs and aging facilities; yet it is clearly the old and the decayed that characterize the city, that reinforce the continuing exodus, not only of whites but of middle-class Negroes, and that drive those who are financially able to the private and the parochial schools. And where interest turns from public to private education, the focus of other commitments is likely to abandon the public sector as well. For most Americans the school (after form 1040) is the prime source of public concern and action. No one has ever moved out of a place because the streets were poorly paved or the water works inadequate, or even because the cops were believed to be corrupt. But they *will* leave if the schools are poor.

In city after city the exodus continues. A few years ago urban planners spoke hopefully of the return to the center, of a migration back to the core city by people who had had enough of car pools and commuting, of mowing lawns and compulsory neighborliness. But although some came back—most of them people whose children had grown and moved away—the tide never turned. Nevertheless the planners continued to produce their schemes, each of them calling for more ambitious programs in transportation, housing, and general redevelopment. Yet none ever focused on the single public service that must constitute the very essence of urban life and renewal—public education. Many plans have made—and still make—reference to the need for new schools, and some describe—in four colors—where the schools should be located. At the same time they ignore what should go on inside them, how they are to be structured and controlled, how they involve the community, on what schedule they operate, what technology and urban resources they might use, how they are to be financed (and how well), who their students should be, where the teachers and materials will come from, and what they are to do. The conception of the planner, like that of the school administrator, is that education will take place in unitary classrooms filled by thirty students, a teacher, and a few textbooks—the village school renewed year after year in place after place, to an endless, monotonous eternity. Boston's elegant ten-year plan, filled with attractive proposals for redevelopment, for regional centers, and cultural improvement, pays some attention to school buildings but none to what should be going on inside them (presumably this is being left to the School Committee); New York is talking about large campus high schools to mitigate racial segregation problems, and it is now even beginning to discuss a "school for the year 2000." But no one is talking about educational planning as an integral part of urban redevelopment. No one has begun to consider the relation of the transportation grid to the possibilities of educational television and long-distance computerized instruction. (Even now there are scattered experiments in which children can dial a language laboratory from their home telephones.) There has been no thought (at least no public thought) about the relationship of the shrinking work week to the immutable six-hour school day or about the possible connections between the labor surplus in the slums and the desperate need for additional nonprofessional personnel in the schools. A few cities have started to employ teacher aides and "room mothers" recruited in the local community, but none does it systematically in all schools. There have been few thorough studies of the relationship between the welfare burden and the increased cost of better education. There has been no examination of the possibility that in a crowded city the population is sufficiently dense to enable a child to attend not one school each week or each year, but a different one every day of the week, each with its own special services and facilities, that, indeed, a whole neighborhood—or the whole city—can become a campus, and not merely the object of an occasional field trip. There has been no consideration given the possibility of integrating children one or two or three days a week in special schools with special English courses, or in up-to-date technical training, or in foreign language instruction or in a dozen other kinds of prestige-laden special programs which could mitigate the fears of white parents. There has been no study of the possibility that the school cafeteria can be made sufficiently attractive and accessible to draw parents and the general community for lunch with the children. (If they are too dreadful for adults, then they are too dreadful for children as well.) There has been little consideration given the idea of installing branch public libraries inside the schools, or of subsidizing beginning painters and sculptors and dancers to practice their art in studios provided in the school building. (If the colleges have become major patrons of the arts, why shouldn't the public schools?) There has been no thought given the idea that attractive shops for special craftsmen—ceramicists, potters, jewelers—could be built right into new schools and made available at reasonable rent (or no rent) provided the craftsmen make themselves available at specified hours to the children studying around them. There has been no serious discussion of how the schools could systematically be used as levers for social change in the neighborhood, of ways that they can become community centers offering not only night classes and library facilities, but sponsoring community theater, neighborhood jazz concerts, family reading groups, and dedicating themselves to a general hospitality toward all neighborhood groups who wish to use their facilities. There has been no serious effort made to give the local community a determining voice in establishing curricula and in deciding how a school building should be used. (Except for a few isolated instances: in New York, for example, a group of parents recently asked for such a voice in the affairs of a new intermediate school in Harlem, including a veto on the teachers to be assigned there.) There has been no full study of the school tax inequities between the city and the affluent suburbs, no examination of how the complete metropolitan region can work together in school planning and in the development of collaborative resources, not even a suggestion that city and suburban administrators and teachers might now and again talk to each other—something they rarely do now. No planner, in the schools or in the planning departments, has ever tried to calculate the relationship (if any) between the school budget and the dropout rate, has ever attempted to assess the tax costs and the ultimate savings in welfare expenses and police protection of an educational system in which *everyone* gets a full twelve years of training, and in which most get at least two beyond that. We have extensive data on highway use, on land development, and the real estate market, but we know almost nothing about the intimate relationship between educational quality and the economic and social future of the city—indeed of the whole nation. No one in America knows how much it costs to run a good urban school system.

* * *

And perhaps no one wants to know. Every major school department issues mountains of statistics on enrollment, on the number of teachers and students, school lunches served, classes for the handicapped, costs of transportation, attendance and truancy, and

on almost everything else that does not relate to actual performance. But to get the mean reading scores for a particular school
or district, to determine accurately the number of dropouts and to
learn what they do after they leave school, even to discover how
well a particular school does in placing the graduates of its vocational programs—to learn these things is like dealing with the
secret police. If the statistics are kept at all—and often, even if
they exist, they are not compiled—they are rarely made public.
By refusing to confess its own failures the system succeeds in embarrassing and intimidating the conscientious parents and in driv-
ing off the rest. "You know your child can't read and write," a
Chicago mother confided, "but you think it's just your kid reflecting your own inadequacies. You think he's a freak, so you
don't say anything. It wasn't until someone stole some of the reading scores from one of the schools around here that we discovered
that everyone in this neighborhood was in the same boat."

The schools of the city—and in many other American communities—are still run on a premise of success: failures are implicit-
ly attributed to the child, to the community—to almost anything
but the system itself. At the same time the system takes credit for
motivating children, for interesting them in normal classroom
activities, and for the long list of accomplishments with which
history has always complimented public education. By not pub-
lishing data on performance—except for the most superficial self-
serving statistics—the schools can have it both ways. They can
take credit for success and blame failure somewhere else. And by
so doing they reinforce the comfortable public notion that nothing
is very seriously wrong, that a competent hierarchy is administer-
ing its funds wisely, and that limited budgets—while not ample
—are generally sufficient to maintain reasonably adequate standards.

The fact is that most of the schools of the city are not urban but
village schools; they are organized as if the children they served
were scattered thinly across vast geographical areas, and they operate on social, intellectual, and moral premises more characteristic
of the nineteenth century than of the twentieth. Most of them are
still engaged in attempts to impart information at a time when
television, tapes, books, magazines, and other media can commu-
nicate most data at least as effectively as the vocal cords of the

teacher. They have not really begun to take advantage of the technology of this culture, nor have they recognized that genuine education must now deal more with process than with "facts," more with styles of thought, with ways of asking and answering questions and solving problems, than with bodies of material. Facts are highly perishable, and their half life becomes shorter every year. Education consequently must be oriented to techniques, to modes of learning, and to developing the individual's confidence in his ability to master the world—to master the society, the technology, the complexities that life throws up to him. It must be oriented to a sense that anything can be learned, and that the learning is worthwhile. It can no longer force a fourteen-year-old to choose which facts and skills he wishes to learn, and which he wants to forego for the rest of his life, can no longer make him select either the vocational program, the academic program, or some sort of "general" program tailored to nothing at all. No school, no system, can consider its programs as terminal. In this culture, the education that is not open-ended, that does not allow —indeed encourage—further education, is not education at all.

The village schools of the city are, on the whole, rigid, obsolete, and often irrelevant; and their performance, given the urgent cultural insistence on education, is a disaster. Of any generation of seventh graders, 85 percent *do not* complete four years of college; 75 percent do not even begin college. In any ghetto area more than half never finish high school, and even those who do are often handed worthless diplomas that symbolize nothing but the student's staying power and the system's condescension. Denying or disregarding these limitations, the schools continue to operate as if nothing were seriously wrong, while the systems that administer them function not to foster change but to impede it. Their constants are budgets, political accommodation, and established administrative routines; all programs, all educational ideas are fitted to them. Financially they are premised on an economy of scarcity, on productive resources sharply limited by shortages of capital, manpower, and time. Thus their basic education is backward. Rather than beginning with educational necessity and acting as if the society were sufficiently affluent to meet that necessity, they start—and end—with the paltry resources that absentee ownership and local tax consciousness are willing to grant. Every lake in this wealthy country is jammed with motorboats and waterskiers, every highway lined with automobiles, but the schools are abandoned at three every afternoon, and the parks at dusk, because the public treasury is assertedly too weak to sustain better service.

The resources exist, but they still flow in overwhelming abundance to the private sector and to the communities that least need them. They flow to the suburbs and to the great establishments of private wealth; and every year, despite the apparently increasing programs of public welfare, the inequities become greater. If we really mean to have effective *public* education, then urban and suburban systems can no longer operate as independent enterprises each with its separate and unequal local financial capabilities, its own special, and often limited facilities, its own little circumscribed area of concern. The problems of segregation and financing have already spilled from the city to the suburbs—to New Rochelle and Englewood and Malverne—and it is clear that they will spill more in the future. They are no longer subject to containment. At the same time the educational cripples, the welfare cases, the incompetent, the hostile—they will be with us forever. They do not respect political boundaries and geographic limits. Suburban isolation is but a temporary luxury; ultimately the agony of the city will make itself felt in the periphery as well. There is, moreover, no academic rationale for the maintenance of clusters of hundreds of independent little school districts in a single metropolitan region; what they can do separately in integrating schools, in financing them, in planning and operating programs, they can do far more effectively together. The only educational reason for their separation is the perpetuation of segregation and inequity. At the same time there is no reason why large units cannot be subdivided into smaller districts-within-districts to give local communities a greater measure of control in the determination of individual school programs and policy—why the doors of the school cannot be open to any individual or group in the community, and to any ideas, no matter how revolutionary. Central administrations can provide the expertise, can staff and organize the programs, and can articulate the options available. But the people who are served by the schools are—or should be—more than clients. The schools are theirs, and there is no reason why they should not have the major voice in exercising the educational options available to them.

The resources exist. But they have not been mobilized. The federal government has now been committed, at least in theory, to the support of public education. In 1965–66 more than one billion dollars went to the public schools under the Elementary and Secondary Education Act. But so far the commitment has been too cautious, too tentative, to make a substantial difference. Not enough money has been allocated, and what has been allocated often went to the wrong people through the wrong channels. While superintendents and politicians (who are collecting all the money) warn of federal control, the real danger is that the money will make no difference at all, that it will merely reinforce the existing hierarchies and the machines that are creating the problems in the first place. The schools do not require aid nearly as much as do children and education, and until far greater influence is exercised by the parents and those most beholden to public education, most of the new money will make no impact at all. Writing in the magazine *The Public Interest*, Christopher Jencks recently suggested that all funds for education be distributed to parents or children to use for tuition in private educational institutions competing for clients on the open market. It is his feeling that the public school has already outlived its usefulness and that America should replace it with a system of private education. His proposal, however, has merit even if the public system is maintained. If the clients of the schools were able to take their federal money to those public establishments they wished to attend, or have their children attend, then clearly efforts would be made to attract them. If all the funds allocated under Title I of the Elementary and Secondary Education Act for culturally deprived areas had been issued directly to parents for designation to those educational institutions their children attend, then schools and systems might have acted much more swiftly to upgrade the rundown classes and buildings and programs they now offer their slum communities. If every deprived child represented a bonus, not to the system, but to the school in which he decided to study, his political and educational impotence would be substantially mitigated.

The state of urban education has gone beyond the point where it is possible to think of particular problems requiring solution.

The city schools are not healthy enterprises requiring first aid. They are structurally unsound, because they are too old and rigid to serve their social purpose. Urban education—given what now exists—is essentially a new social function that requires new implementation and that will, in most major cities, involve the abandonment of a major part of the machinery that now passes as public education—buildings, books, administrative routines, and personnel. While it is clearly impossible to scrap all existing resources, there is no logic in reproducing them year after year. Educational problems vary from place to place depending on population density, geographical conditions, and social situation; yet clearly the time has come when every metropolitan area must ask itself what it would do if it had no buildings, no central administration, no hierarchy on Beacon Street or Livingston Street or North LaSalle Street, what it would do if it did not even have a corps of teachers. Would it reproduce the existing system? Would it start all over erecting factories and prisons and call them neighborhood schools? How would it organize education? What would it teach? What resources would it employ? What would Boston or New York or Chicago do if they had to start from scratch? What kind of education could be planned, not by the superintendent of schools, but by the imaginative people of the community?

In the past generation we have overhauled our highways, our war machine, our airlines, and airplanes, our downtown office buildings, our very style of life. But we have hardly begun to overhaul our urban schools. Most of the school plant dates back a good generation while educational ideas in the schools have changed hardly at all since the nineteenth century. But where the older America—which shaped public education—provided alternatives to successful formal schooling, modern America does not. The shop, the farm, the open spaces are gone. For better or worse, education now has to do it all. Academic necessity, the ailments of the city, the demands of the technology, the pressures of racial and social change, all demand the kind of candid appraisal that few schools have received. They demand infusions of new funds and new ideas. They demand a fundamental restructuring of the system itself, and they require a degree of community involvement and accessibility that is denied to most people in most cities. They demand a totally new approach distinct from the concept of the unitary class in the unitary school, and they demand the utilization of all the urban and technological resources now becoming available.

Ultimately the issue of urban education is also the issue of the morale and life of the city itself. The schools have supplanted the market place as the focus of the community. They, not the subways or the sewer system, tie the city together. If they fail—as they are failing—then the community will disintegrate into a congeries of suburbs and renaissance baronies separated by ghettoes and violence. If they fail, then the public weal will forever be committed to an uneasy division between warfare and welfare, while those sectors of public activity that make life rich and meaningful —the arts, recreation, education, the beauty of the city and country—will become ever more privately glorious and publicly neglected. If they fail, then urban life fails, too.